Preface

We did not sit down and plan to write a book together. Of course, eventually, we sat down and met many times, usually with a Yello Sub sandwich in our hands. But in the beginning, neither of us expected our work to become a book.

Yet six years ago, when each of us felt called to separate doctor of ministry degrees at separate seminaries, the Spirit put us on a path toward a shared project and a shared passion. Each of our degrees concluded with our dissertations—one on congregations' decision-making processes (Tim's) and the other on preaching amid controversy and conflict within the congregation (Matt's).

After graduation Tim published a two-part article online at Good Faith Media, summarizing his conclusions regarding churches dealing with same-sex marriage.[1] At that point, we began working to combine our research to publish another article. In frustration we concluded that there was just too much information to pare down into a single article. Then the Spirit moved, and Matt said, "Then let's shoot for the moon and make it a book!"

"Great idea!" Tim responded. That was the beginning of more hard work—studying, creating, writing, negotiating, head-butting, dealing with emotional turmoil, and more writing and rewriting. Judson Press saw the value in what we were saying and challenged us to broaden our focus to include more diverse churches and consult with church leaders who had more varied experiences than we did. They represented churches with more diversity and inclusion than the churches in our initial studies, and we are thankful for this broadened scope and larger collection of voices. In chapter 8 we include some writings by these participants in our research process. Doing the research and writing this book has been a tremendous learning adventure for us, even if we did have days when we wondered if this project would ever make it to print! In these pages, you will find heartbreak and hope, new and old ideas, and the fruit of a journey in which two authors had to learn to trust God and one another.

But why this topic, and why now? What do our voices add to the conversation as congregations work to navigate the cultural and political controversies of our current context? Our hope is that we might provide a broader background and several perspectives as we share data from multiple churches and voices from both laypersons and clergy. Tim's previous professional degrees were in developmental and clinical psychology, and Matt's were in psychology and ministry. Matt also had training as a chaplain. From those perspectives, we invite readers to examine the work of the church through various lenses, including congregational *polity*, the work of *preaching*, and healthy church *process*. Underlying it all is the need for authenticity and faith to build trust.

Trust and trust-building are essential parts of a vibrant, growing church community, which we call an elastic or adaptive church. The 2015 *Obergefell v. Hodges* decision provided an important backdrop for our academic work and for this book. We hope that regardless of the potentially divisive issue they face, congregations can engage in the work of trust. As we explore the journeys of churches that have approached the reality of the Supreme Court decision to legalize same-sex marriage, we ask how congregations might practice and share trust together. The church has weathered many tragic storms over the centuries, and its message and purpose will continue into the future. Thus, we are excited by the bright future we see for God's churches, knowing that they will not look like churches of the past but will be elastic and adaptive—stretching and engaging to meet the needs of all persons in their communities. In the same way the Spirit brought about creative work through the two of us via our individual and shared conversations over these last six years, we believe the Spirit is at work in the conversations of your congregations. So, let's start the journey!

NOTES

1. Timothy J. Bonner, "Your Church and Same-Gender Marriage—Part 1," Good Faith Media, January 4, 2021, https://goodfaithmedia.org/your-church-and-same-gender-marriage-part-1/; Bonner, "Your Church and Same-Gender Marriage—Part 2," Good Faith Media, January 5, 2021, https://goodfaithmedia.org/your-church-and-same-gender-marriage-part-2/.

1

Congregations and Controversy[1]

As M. Craig Barnes wrote in 2016, "Congregations had better be worried about what divides them."[2] As we find our postmodern society in disequilibrium, Christian congregations are losing numbers and energy due to a variety of circumstances. Political upheaval and polarization. The COVID-19 pandemic and widely divergent responses. Radical social changes, especially around issues of race and sexuality. Media that is motivated to divide rather than unite. With this ever-increasing complexity, is it any wonder that American churches are finding themselves struggling to understand the world and connect? These political and ideological divisions threaten to divide institutions, families, and congregations, leading to a growing distrust of those who represent opposing viewpoints.

In the past, congregations were able to share unity in commonly held religious beliefs, but Princeton Theological Seminary president M. Craig Barnes and others suggest that those days are over. Following the 2016 US presidential election, he wrote, "The pastors I fret over the most are those whose congregations are divided in their political allegiances. These churches pride themselves on being a place where all types of diversity are held together by a common center in Christ. 'The center will always hold,' pastors have said for years. But this last election revealed that we have never been a centered country; congregations had better be worried about what divides them."[3]

The 2020 election cycle, surrounded by a global pandemic and heightened anxiety, did nothing but exacerbate the problem. Congregations divided by political party now found themselves divided over if and when to meet in person, whether to wear masks in worship, and how to talk about vaccines. Churches had a new set of divisive issues to worry about.

Who Are We?

This divisiveness reveals that something deeper is at stake than simply the latest controversy or political tiff. In the past, Christians *named their faith as their primary identity*. We were Christians first, or "church people." That identity marker, though, has largely been replaced by political divisions with increased polarization. Now many of us church people are first and foremost "red people"—conservatives or traditionalists (some of our intellectual friends prefer to be called libertarians) who favor the status quo and remain loyal to "the way things used to be." We hearken back to a day when things seemed clearer, more upright, and perhaps easier. We support leaders and culture makers who wish to return to those days or at least grieve the fact that we have left them. We remember the days in which hard work, individual effort, self-sufficiency, and family values were believed to be all that were necessary to live successfully. In terms of our government, we believe that less government is better than more government until it isn't. Government policies affecting our economic lives and business interests are seen as dangerous overreaches, but policies that govern our personal lives (e.g., marriage restriction, abortion prohibition, and prayer in public schools) are seen as commonsense protections of American values. In terms of our faith and faith communities, many of us red people remember a day when the country was more homogeneous and less pluralistic. Our culture and the church went hand in hand in defending those values. As a general rule, we mistrust those who are blue and paint them as coercive, valueless, and dangerous.

Meanwhile, many of us are first and foremost "blue people"—liberals (some of our intellectual friends prefer to be called progressives) in favor of transformation and communal change. We, too, remember "the good old days," but we remember them as less good for people of color, women, or anyone who stepped outside the set norm of society and group expectations. We support leaders and culture makers who wish to bring about a new day and more progressive policies focusing on alterity to protect the "other" and the marginalized. We hope for a day in which communities set aside the "-isms" that limit and categorize us, and learn to value one another, even those who are different, as equals. In terms of our government, we believe that more government is better than less government until it isn't. Government policies in our personal lives (e.g., concerning marriage, faith practice, or a woman's right to govern her own body) are seen as dangerous overreaches, but policies that govern our economic lives and business interests are commonsense protections that help bring about a more equitable society. In terms of our faith and faith communities, many of us blue people have chosen to step away from faith or "organized religion" in part or whole. Those who have stayed committed to a faith group do so largely in ways that emphasize personal transformation, collaboration, social justice, and community development. Many blue Christian preachers deliver sermons that acknowledge white-Christian guilt for the ways some have benefited from an oppressive history. We invite our congregations to recognize and empower those on the margins of society. Generally, we mistrust those who are red and paint them as coercive, valueless, and dangerous.

Given these disparate perspectives, the results of a Pew study a few years ago will likely not be surprising. Democrats and Republicans were each asked about members of the other party and to compare them to other Americans. Various adjectives were given as options, and the adjectives that both parties used to describe members of the other party were strikingly similar. "Unintelligent" was in the top five for each party; "immoral" was in the top three for each; and the top adjective that each party gave the other was "closed-minded."[4]

It's Not Easy Being Purple

Barnes worries most about those churches that straddle the line between red and blue, often referred to as "purple churches." Colorado pastor and ecumenical leader James R. Ryan defines such churches: "Purple congregations are made up of some folks who are very liberal when it comes to political and theological perspectives and some who are very conservative, but a majority of the members of purple congregations would identify themselves as moderates. Maybe they are a light pink or maybe a pale blue. On the continuum between red and blue, they would place themselves somewhere in the middle half."[5] Churches filled with those in the "middle half," as well as those delicately balancing both red and blue, seem to be the ones Barnes is concerned about. Those who attempt to find a middle ground, or include both red and blue ideologies, face more challenges than ever before. Our culture's division and divisiveness make it difficult to create an institution of commitment to Christ that is free from political identity and language. Churches increasingly find themselves losing members from one camp or the other while struggling to stay faithful to their Christian morals and nonpolitical history.

Of course, even congregations that identify as mostly liberal or mostly conservative often represent a similarly sized range on the ideological spectrum. Differences of opinion exist between those who represent various shades of blue or shades of red. Controversies in churches are as old as the church itself; indeed, since human beings have gathered, sociological, cultural, and spiritual forces have driven them apart. Seemingly, those who straddle the line between red and blue have a particularly challenging road before them. Ryan agrees. He suggests "this division between the reds and the blues is broader than just scriptural interpretation or power struggles. Scriptural interpretation is a symptom of the division rather than the cause. I now believe that this division has more to do with the overall 'worldview,' or more specifically, what I would call 'faith view.'"[6] This suggests why purple congregations have a particular struggle. When a congregation straddles that line, tension exists.

A deep fracture separates reds and blues, which we can see by surveying the culture around us. Americans can find institutions and structures that support and reinforce their worldview of choice. The news media a person chooses to consume fortifies his or her position. Social media insiders have acknowledged that their platforms are designed to increase this divide.[7] Even decisions such as what state to reside in, which community to live in, and which school district to send one's children to help to reinforce Americans' worldviews. David Sipress takes the point to the ludicrous with his political cartoon from 2017, showing a couple sitting on the couch watching the weather forecast on the news, while the announcer narrates, "That was Brad with the Democratic weather. Now here's Tammy with the Republican weather."[8] Ludicrous perhaps, but various media's treatment of scientific topics such as climate change and its impact on our weather suggests that even the local meteorology report is not off-limits for politicization.

The proliferation of institutional and media-driven polarization means that there is often little room for the middle ground that Barnes and Ryan describe. Thus, the implicit question they ask is a valid one: *Will the church follow suit, or is there a model for purple churches that allows them to survive, navigate, and perhaps even thrive amid such polarized worldviews?*

Our Own Purple Stories

We, as authors, care deeply about this question. We acknowledge that ours is not the first nor the most profound description of these fundamental differences in American congregations. Yet we have personally seen what this division can do in a congregational context. Both of us have experienced and shared the concern that Barnes and Ryan have noted. Combined, we have spent decades engaged in or employed by churches that might be considered "purple." We have lived through this division at both a professional and personal level. We have seen firsthand the shift that Barnes named and have shared his concern.

In the last few years alone, churches have faced significant division over abortion, gun control, tax policies, civil rights as they relate to race and sexuality, COVID-19 restrictions, vaccination, and a host of other issues. Every time a new controversial law or bill crosses a governor's desk or the Supreme Court's docket, disagreements and arguments ensue in Bible study groups, church councils, and denominational resolution committees.

Perhaps the most significant dividing line in recent years has been the splintering around same-sex marriages. A benchmark came in 2015 with the US Supreme Court *Obergefell v. Hodges* decision that legalized same-sex marriages. The issue had been settled legally for the whole nation. However, it was of major consequence for all the churches in which weddings were taking place. In general, the court ruling reverberated throughout the leadership of many congregations, creating much worrisome tension, anxiety, and in some cases repulsion with incumbent anger. Regardless of their beliefs, biblical interpretations, policies, or traditions, all churches had to deal with it in one way or another—directly or indirectly. The Supreme Court decision complicated the church landscape and presented one of the greatest challenges for Christian congregations today. Many congregations, especially those largely blue or red, experienced minimal conflict. Many progressive churches cheered the decision and happily began conducting same-sex weddings in their sanctuaries immediately. Many conservative churches denounced the decision and proclaimed with statements and policy revisions that such ceremonies would not be allowed in their sanctuaries or by staff members employed by their churches. Many Christians and churches, however, found themselves in the middle. Long able to ignore the question due to an inability to conduct legal weddings in their states, they were now brought to a crisis of ideology and faith. Individual Christians, purple congregations, and entire denominations found themselves straddling a line on this significant cultural touch point. Those who had long held the middle found themselves engaged in conversations about sexual behaviors and marriage. As we have seen, this engagement can be healthy and constructive—but it also has the potential to release significant divisive anger, distrust, resentment, and even hostility, which are addressed in this volume.

Meanwhile, we have lived through this division at an academic level as well. In the years following the *Obergefell v. Hodges* ruling, both of us were engaged in doctor of ministry programs (at different institutions). Yet, through these parallel academic journeys, we were arriving at similar findings. Specifically relating to conversations around same-sex marriage, we began to see congregations that were doing some healthy and thoughtful work. Such work was not without disagreement or pain but helped them to stretch and adapt.

In this book, we share some of our insights and questions as well as our vision for the future of the church. We hope that churches, congregation leaders, pastors, and individual Christians might pick up our work and add their voices to the mix and that together we might seek holy wisdom for our current age. As many of us share our own purple stories, we begin to find answers together. Meanwhile we recognize that this story is not only ours but God's. We have seen God at work through the hard conversations in which congregations engage. Through our listening, learning, and trusting, God is honored and present (see the Communication Covenant in chapter 7).

While we have seen congregational struggles, we also have success stories. Through both academic and personal lenses, we have seen healthy processes, strong leadership, and hopeful strategies for the divided congregations in our midst. Particularly, we have seen congregations face questions about same-sex marriage and LGBTQ+[9] leadership and grow through the process. In the pages ahead, we hope to explore the health and vitality of congregations and the role of pastors and lay leaders in the body of Christ today. We again ask the question, perhaps more explicitly in the pages ahead, *Are there guidelines and principles for churches that allow them to survive, navigate, and perhaps even thrive amid such polarized worldviews?*

Here we offer a word of clarification: we will not suggest in these pages that the only way for a congregation to thrive is to be "purple." We share Barnes's and Ryan's concern that these center churches face specific challenges, given our bifurcated culture. But we hope that all churches, regardless of their ideological makeup, will find in these pages a helpful model for being healthy and thriving. What we call the *elastic, adaptive church* comes in many shapes and sizes and has varying ideologies. Congregations that fall in the center might find these concepts particularly helpful, as they seek to find theological and practical models for churches that allow for hospitality to those on the right and the left. However, we hope that congregations that would define themselves as unabashedly red or proudly blue might also find models for healthy, optimal functioning in these pages. Purpleness is not a prerequisite for an elastic, adaptive church.

The Three *P*'s

Any good preacher knows how to craft a message with three points that all start with the same letter! Of course, this stereotype leads to some sermons that seem to stretch the power of triumvirate alliteration toward incredulity. Yet our combined work and insights have led us to highlight three concepts that do indeed all start with the same letter. In the following pages, we set out to answer three questions that we find relevant to the conversation. (1) Who in the church is engaged when a congregation faces a controversial decision, and what will that engagement look like—*polity*? (2) How may the preacher lead from the pulpit in ways that are faithful to Scripture and congregational ownership of the process—*preaching*? Finally, (3) how do we engage and empower a congregation to make such decisions constructively—*process*? We will explore these three questions leading to three critical insights.

POLITY

The first critical insight to discovering what divides congregations has to do with what unites them. Polity is central to exploring congregational divisions simply because the way in which congregations make important policy decisions must be addressed. Chapter 2 explores the complexity of the issue. With so many denominational structures and principles of polity at play, one cannot begin with many universal assumptions.

Yet the one shared assumption we do argue for is *the importance of trust*. From our perspective, regardless of the structures and polity by which one enters this task of building healthy congregations, a foundation of trust in God, the "other," and the self must be present. In this chapter, we will explore the philosophical underpinnings of trust, examine it from a theological point of view, and then move into a conversation about trust as it is demonstrated in ecclesiology.

Related to trust is the concept of *alterity*. Here we rely heavily on the work of University of Edinburgh theologian Ulrich Schmiedel, who suggests that alterity, or what he calls a radical "openness to otherness"[10] must become the practice of congregations and denominations. It is not a pie-in-the-sky notion. He begins with a warning much like Barnes, bemoaning both a "crisis in the churches" and "churches in crisis."[11] Yet he suggests that this notion of alterity—congregational community based on the conception of trusting others—allows churches to navigate these crises. He suggests that the goal must be an "elasticized ecclesiology," stretching to welcome new ideas—becoming the *elastic, adaptive church*. The chapter concludes by exploring some practical questions regarding polity, denominational structure, and ecclesiological practice as we move into the pragmatic work of congregational decision-making.

PREACHING

What happens from behind the pulpit is also important to the work of healthy congregations. Not only is the role of the staff and professional leadership important for the task of congregational leadership, but preaching is central to that leadership. How might pastoral conversations—and, most crucially, the sermonic event—develop and strengthen that trust, moving us beyond either divisive bifurcation or avoidance of difficult issues altogether? How might the preaching of trust in God and the other move the congregation's decision-making process toward mutually trusting relationships, honest engagement, unanimity, and welcoming of all for the expansion of the body of Christ?

Chapter 3 provides several metaphors for congregational communication and engagement. You are invited to think of which best describes your church and to consider whether that is the type of church you want to be.

In chapter 4, we delve into how the concept of alterity impacts the work of the pulpit, exploring a conversational ecclesiology that uses open dialogue in an intentional preaching process. Perkins School of Theology homiletician O. Wesley Allen's concept of a "homiletic of all believers"[12] deeply informs this process, and we share how he and other homileticians reveal a shared homiletic based on alterity. We examine the preaching task as it relates to community, story, content, and form, alongside church historian and scholar Martin Marty's invitation to build trust in congregations.

PROCESS

The process utilized in decision-making makes a crucial difference. Reflecting on Schmiedel's *elasticized ecclesiology*, we show in the next few chapters what is at stake in churches if we are to be/become the body of Christ. Our examination of *process* begins in chapter 5 where we address the current challenges for churches by providing successful strategies we have learned. There we introduce the Cycle of Building Trust Model and a "packing list" that provides general guidelines for action. These tools help to provide a big-picture perspective on developing healthy, strong, growing churches.

Chapter 6 continues our exploration with the presentation of three *composite church models* that help to ask our second driving question: *How can we engage and empower a congregation to make hard decisions?* We offer a strengths-based model, suggesting that different congregations might find divergent—but each functional in its own way—models for congregational decision-making. All the congregations we studied embarked on "journeys of trust" but did so in very different ways.

We have researched churches and consulted with church leaders from coast to coast in North America. Some of those church leaders have performed same-sex weddings and some have not. We cover churches with numerous LGBTQ+ participants and churches that have next to none who publicly share that identity. We also share vignettes from churches whose processes were outside of our example churches.

You may still be wondering, *How did our model churches respond? What did they do that worked well, and what did they do that did not? What was the outcome of their journey? What are the potholes and cliffs along the way? Where can the downhill, open-road path be found? How can we best deal with divisive controversies in our faith community?* Answers to these questions are found in chapter 6, which gives a full, chronological account of three churches' decision-making processes and their outcomes.

In the first composite church, which we named Eastern Harbor Church, the personnel worked intentionally to include minorities, including LGBTQ+ folks, despite the personal opinions of church members that covered the whole spectrum of possibilities. In another church model, which we called West Bay Christian Church, a lead pastor patiently led the whole congregation to a near-consensus decision on how they would respond to the new same-sex marriage law of the land. The third example is Journey Community Church, which initiated a long, lay-led process in their attempt to grasp how they could best respond to the highly emotion-charged question "Do we have 'gay weddings' or not?" Their congregation's lengthy decision-making process answered that question.

We discuss in chapter 7 the communication and group facilitation *tools* necessary for churches in transition or considering adapting to social changes and competing demands for our attention in our postmodern society. That chapter continues with what we have learned on our journey. We provide guidelines for managing the process and suggestions for answering how-to questions. The Communication Covenant provides a very specific recipe for achieving excellent, constructive dialogue with empathetic listening as well as emotionally astute speaking. This chapter also includes Guidelines for Healthy Trust-Building Discussions, which are necessary for maintaining boundaries and protecting egos during any group process activity in the decision-making journey. Furthermore, the guidance in this chapter can help prevent misunderstandings, emotional escalation, and increased animosity or division in congregations undertaking a process of considering and addressing changes.

We have intended to be considerate and inclusive of all viewpoints—conservative, liberal, and the many in between. We do not advocate or promote any particular stance, position, or decision-making process—that is left for you to decide what works for your context. Our experiences and research show that whatever path you take, the process risks being highly problematic, emotion-filled, potentially explosive, and divisive. We offer insights based on real-life experiences and general guidelines that can apply to any controversial and challenging decision-making process.

Welcome to the Journey!

As two white males, we recognize we have implicit biases and privileges. Our goal in this book is not to deliver all the right answers but to share our voices in the conversation, knowing that diverse others have much to share. Therefore, we have included chapter 8, "Other Voices," which contains the voices of other persons, female and male, who have experienced divisive congregational processes. These clergy and lay leaders provided valuable insights. We include vignettes and essays of their contributions, allowing them to give perspectives on both successes and failures of their congregations' dealing with controversial issues.

Finally, in the last chapter, we reflect on our initial question: *Is there a model for churches that allows them to survive, navigate, and perhaps even thrive amid polarized worldviews?* We offer principles and practical suggestions, ending with guidelines for developing trust within a congregation, even one facing controversy.

We guess that you have read this far because you, too, yearn for answers to these big questions regarding controversial issues in faith communities. Perhaps you are a church leader looking for guidance. Maybe you are a pastor searching for a resource. You may be a congregation member without a title or position but have seen a bifurcated, hurting church, and you are unsure where to start the healing process. In the pages ahead, we hope to open the door for hard conversations in congregations, whether the topic at hand is same-sex marriage, racial or gender equality issues, mask-wearing requirements in worship services, congregational approaches to abortion, or any other of a host of controversial issues and ideas that threaten to divide us. In so doing, our hope is not simply to "hold the middle" but to provide a model of "body of Christ elasticity" that allows congregations to build trust, survive, grow, and even thrive through the crises they face. If you are ready to share that task with us, welcome to the journey!

NOTES

1. This chapter relies heavily on material from a previously unpublished thesis: Matthew B. Sturtevant, "The Red and Blue Body of Christ: Preaching Trust of God and Other in a Purple Church" (DMin thesis, Chicago Theological Seminary, 2019), 1–9.

2. M. Craig Barnes, "The Pastors I Worry About," *Christian Century*, January 4, 2017, 35.

3. Barnes, 35.

4. "Partisanship and Political Animosity in 2016," Pew Research Center, June 22, 2016, https://www.pewresearch.org/politics/2016/06/22/partisanship-and-political-animosity-in-2016/.

5. James Ryan, *Doing Justice in a Purple Congregation* (Denver: Colorado Council of Churches, 2008), 8.

6. Ryan, 10.

7. Bobby Allyn, "Here Are 4 Key Points from the Facebook Whistleblower's Testimony on Capitol Hill," NPR.org, updated October 5, 2021, https://www.npr.org/2021/10/05/1043377310/facebook-whistleblower-frances-haugen-congress.

8. David Sipress, "That Was Brad with the Democratic Weather. Now Here's Tammy with the Republican Weather" (cartoon), fineartamerica, March 12, 2017, https://fineartamerica.com/featured/that-was-brad-with-the-democratic-weather-now-david-sipress.html.

9. We acknowledge an ever-evolving spectrum of identities embraced by queer folk, including lesbian, gay, bisexual, transgender, queer/questioning, intersex, and allies. While there is no perfect set of abbreviations, we have chosen to use "LGBTQ+" throughout this work.

10. Ulrich Schmiedel, *Elasticized Ecclesiology: The Concept of Community after Ernst Troeltsch* (Munich: Palgrave Macmillan, 2017), 22.

11. Schmiedel, 1.

12. O. Wesley Allen, *The Homiletic of All Believers: A Conversational Approach to Proclamation and Preaching* (Louisville: Westminster John Knox, 2005).

2

Why Trust? Polity and the Adaptive Church[1]

The priest stands before the congregation, explaining that the diocese leadership has announced a slate of COVID-19 restrictions, including live stream—only worship and masks required in small groups. One parishioner, feeling that the church is caught up in a political distraction, angrily confronts the priest following the service. The priest, who happens to agree with the parishioner, shrugs his shoulders and says, "My hands are tied."

The closed-door staff meeting is contentious. Under debate is whether the church will choose to host a rally sponsored by a pro-life organization. While there is room for disagreement around the staff table, by the time the decision is made, it is final. As they leave the room, all agree that they will present a united front before the congregation.

A congregation is divided on whether to hire an openly gay staff person. Some support the hire, while others are vehemently opposed to it. According to the congregation's polity, every member has a vote on whether the person will be hired. In the weeks leading up to the vote, a host of emails are sent and phone calls are made, as congregation members work to persuade their fellow congregants to agree with their perspective.

"According to the polity of the congregation . . ." That phrase alone has been at the heart of many a church crisis. The polity of any given congregation or denomination has a lot to say about the way controversial issues are addressed and divisive decisions are made. Who will work at the church? What study materials will be used? Which social or political issues will be addressed in our church's statement of belief, mission statement, or identity statement (if there even is one)? What community organizations are allowed to use the church building, and what oversight does the church have regarding its ideology? Who will be baptized? Married? Ordained? Allowed to become a member, teacher, or church leader? These practical questions and issues often become touchpoints to larger cultural and ideological questions.

Of course, these are not entirely new questions. Predominantly white churches during the civil rights era were divided over whether a Black family could become members. Plenty of parishioners left churches when a divorced pastor was chosen to fill the pulpit. Members of Protestant congregations have become apoplectic when a parishioner was allowed to marry a Roman Catholic and vice versa. Yet the kind of crisis Schmiedel and Barnes speak of seems to have a heightened level of anxiety in our current context. Especially among those churches divided between red and blue, deep divisions outside of the church infiltrate pews and Sunday school rooms inside the church.

Thus, questions of polity must also be heightened. We cannot begin with a conversation about the *how* without first addressing the *who*. Who will answer questions such as those above? Who will set and enact policy and practice? Who is in charge around here, anyway? Polity and polarization are two dynamics inextricably intertwined.

A Few Words about Polity

Clearly, differences in polity and ideology have led congregations and denominations to address issues around LGBTQ+ persons in a host of different ways. A comparative polity course in a seminary curriculum might do well to study a denominational survey of responses to LGBTQ+ issues, as a case study about the "Who's in charge around here?" question. While we see the value in such an approach to compare, contrast, and divide the Christian religious experience into various denominational "distinctives," we have a different goal in mind.

For much of the last three hundred years of American religious study, discussions about polity have often been exercises in categorizing, comparing, and contrasting denominational structures. When we speak of polity, we are really asking, "Yes, but what kind of Christian are you? Catholic or Protestant? Independent or denominational? Congregational or connectional? Top-down or bottom-up?" We have done this for some good reasons because denominations and congregations do indeed govern themselves in different ways. When it comes to understanding who makes decisions regarding divisive issues in a congregation, methods of governance still matter. For example, the ways independent, congregationally governed bodies like Baptist churches will determine if they will marry a same-sex couple or ordain a person identifying as LGBTQ+ are fundamentally different from the way an international body like the United Methodist Church or Roman Catholic Church will hold such a conversation. Clearly, there are indeed distinctions in the ways that various congregations will discuss and approach divisive issues.

Yet, while not irrelevant, these questions are perhaps less relevant than they once were. To the average churchgoer, denominational identity now seems less valuable than it has for several centuries. Even on an academic level, the study of congregations has tended to see more similarities in polity than distinctives. More than twenty years ago, sociologist of religion Nancy Ammerman and colleagues published a handbook meant to aid the study of congregations, which recognized this:

> *The fact that most religious participation in this country is voluntary, not legally obligatory; collective, not individualized; and popular, not the preserve of an elite, has meant that American people of faith have tended to organize themselves into congregations. The congregational form—local, voluntary, lay-led, religious*

assemblies—is an ancient and hallowed norm in Baptist, Jewish, and Congregational traditions, but over the history of the United States and for various reasons, it has been adopted into the polity of other traditions. Indeed, a pattern of de facto congregationalism, the unofficial yet persistent adoption of congregational forms, is increasingly prevalent, even in traditions such as the Presbyterian, Methodist, and Episcopal, where it is not the official norm. Even the US Roman Catholic Church has seen its geographic parish system altered by the assertion of lay people's right to attend the (Catholic) church of their choice.[2]

Ammerman suggests that the American religious experience is a nearly universal congregational one.

We agree there is value in recognizing and exploring the reality that Christians tend to gather in local congregations. Yet there is still a value in examining this "de facto congregationalism" that is still largely present today. Regardless of denominational polity, local congregations find themselves facing questions tinged with political divisiveness. A Methodist congregation must consider whether they should join the local Black Lives Matter chapter. An Episcopal parish considers whether to display a No Guns Allowed sign on their front door in a concealed-carry state. A Presbyterian congregation is divided on whether to sell its property to a nonprofit working to build affordable housing. An independent evangelical church faces the question of what to do when one of its staff members announces he is gay and wants to be married in the church.

While we hope others are fervently writing about how to discuss controversial issues within larger, international denominational structures and how to bring grace and trust into those conversations, we focus on decisions and conversations taking place *within* local congregations. It is likely that you, dear reader, are a part of a local congregation, whether that congregation follows the model Ammerman and colleagues call the historically "congregational form," or the broader movement of "de facto congregationalism." Regardless of what your congregation looks like, our hope is that this chapter will provoke a discussion about who belongs, who decides, and who leads congregations that are facing difficult issues. Hint: *it's all about trust.*

What's Trust Got to Do with It?

The concept of trust undergirds the work of mature and healthy churches, regardless of their polity or denomination. Untrusting churches might split over something as insignificant as the color of the carpet in the parlor, but healthy, trusting congregations can weather many a storm together. Does the laity trust the clergy and vice versa? Are there currents of distrust throughout the congregation? Do leaders trust God, and what does that even look like? In this chapter, we build a theological and ecclesiological foundation of trust that we believe will carry congregations through divisive issues. But what is *trust*, anyway? When we speak of trust in this context, we are talking about our relationship with others and the idea that within the bounds of that relationship, we expect individuals to be honest and honor their commitments. Three practical elements of trust are crucial to our understanding of the term: *vulnerability*, *risk*, and *interpersonal relationality*. Together these three ideas form the building blocks of trust.

Psychologist Daniel Goleman, in *Social Intelligence: The Revolutionary New Science of Human Relationships*, writes that we are wired to connect to one another—*relationality*—and that we do this in two ways.[3] We quickly and automatically make connections through both emotional and intuitive "contagion"—what he calls the *low road* of connection—as well as through neural systems of a deliberate and reasoned *high road*. Trust takes place, then, on both levels. "The high road operates when we intentionally make a judgment of whether someone might be trustworthy. But a continual-amygdala appraisal goes on outside our awareness, regardless of whether we consciously think about the issue. The low road labors to keep us safe."[4] All of our brain's parts work in complex, interconnected ways to shape our level of trust in one another.

This takes us to another key component of the idea of trust: *risk*. Philosopher Katherine Hawley acknowledges the riskiness of trust: "Most of us are all too familiar with the riskiness of trust, having endured faithless lovers, dodgy traders, or conniving colleagues (the unluckiest of us have suffered all three). Yet, we know that when people work together trustingly, they can get a lot more done, to the benefit of all concerned."[5] In other words, if we are truly to trust another, there must be a risk of having that trust betrayed. It is not really trusting if we have a full guarantee that the other will do what we are hoping. Trust puts us "out on a limb," acknowledging the possibility of loss or harm. Trust implies risk.

Thus, this risk leads to the third element of trust: *vulnerability*. If risk is the potential for loss or harm, vulnerability is the intentional lack of protection from that loss or harm, ideally to achieve a greater good. At the core of human trust lies a vulnerability in the face of risk and reward. When we trust, we choose vulnerability despite the risk.

So, are these interrelated concepts of interpersonal connection, risk, and vulnerability present in a divided and divisive world? What does trust have to do with congregations and politics? Social psychologist Jonathan Haidt tackles this question in *The Divided Mind: Why Good People Are Divided by Politics and Religion*. Like Goleman, he writes from the perspective of a social psychologist with considerable experience studying morality and behavior. Haidt has researched the things that divide us, including ways that our brains often pursue that division. Like Goleman, Haidt notes the complex ways that we trust (or fail to trust) each other.[6] He suggests two types of cognition: "intuition and reasoning." While we like to think of ourselves as highly functioning, reasonable, and rational, he suggests that "reason is the servant of the intuitions."[7] His metaphor of the elephant and rider is instructive. Our reasoning capability is like the rider who knows where to go and how to get there, but once the rider gets on top of the elephant, all bets are off! Our intuitive processes include our emotions. That process is like an elephant that goes where it wants to go, minimally guided by our reasoning. Thus, when these intuitive processes are marked by distrust, suspicion and division are not far behind.

Yet, Haidt sees the damage that this division causes to our bodies, our minds, and the very psyche of a nation. He summarizes his measured hope in his book's first few pages: "When I was a teenager I wished for world peace, but now I yearn for a world in which competing ideologies are kept in balance, systems of accountability keep us all from getting away with too much, and fewer people believe that righteous ends justify violent means. Not a very romantic wish, but one that we might actually achieve."[8]

Haidt's work is relevant for a community facing diverging ideologies, such as a congregation. We often find ourselves associating only with those who share *our* worldview, choosing to build relationships with, spend time with, and even worship beside only those who share the same matrix. But from a sociocultural perspective, Haidt hopes we might learn to listen to those who represent different matrixes than our own. When he speaks of "balance," he uses the image of the yin-yang symbol,[9] each side in an ideological divide equally balanced, holding each other accountable and keeping the other from gaining the upper hand. Red recognizes the strengths of blue and blue of red. In fact, red strengthens blue and blue, red. He suggests an ideological dialogue that recognizes the strengths of the other and values the perspective of those with whom we disagree.

Haidt writes about the experience of sitting next to a stranger on an airplane and striking up a conversation (in contrast to the experience that some of us have of trying everything in our power to *avoid* striking up said conversation!). He invites us to consider what it would take to engage and listen to the perspective of this other passenger. Instead of hiding behind our magazine or plugging in earbuds, Haidt suggests the following:

We are deeply intuitive creatures whose gut feelings drive our strategic reasoning. This makes it difficult—but not impossible—to

*connect with those who live in other matrixes, which are often
built on different configurations of the available moral founda-
tions. So the next time you find yourself seated beside someone
from another matrix, give it a try. Don't just jump right in. Don't
bring up morality until you've found a few points of commonality
or in some other way established a bit of trust. . . . We're all stuck
here for a while, so let's try to work it out.*[10]

Haidt's suggestion is hopeful, but how might we reach such a
place within a congregation?

The key word in this quote from Haidt is *trust*. Establishing
a "bit of trust" is central to the process, according to Haidt's
formula for success. Thus, if we are to build health in divided
congregations, perhaps multilayered trust is a key part of the
formula: Haidt's elephant and rider and Goleman's high road of
thoughtful rational discussion partnered with the low road of
intuitive connection.

In this brief survey of the work of philosophers, social scientists, and brain scientists, we are laying the foundation for the
importance of trust, especially the type of trust marked by these
three elements of interpersonal relationality, risk, and vulnerability. But what about theologians? What is the nature of trust
in relation to our understanding of the divine? In the next section, we explore how this conception of trust relates to the ways
we talk about God and the ways we talk about one another in
relation to God.

Trust and Theology

The two-thousand-year-old Christian conversation has always
been tied to the terms of a relationship. The very nature of a
Trinitarian God suggests that Christians understand an inher-
ent relationality that is eternal and foundational. Theologian
Jürgen Moltmann, in his groundbreaking work on the social
Trinity, *The Trinity and the Kingdom*, suggests, "The image of
God must not merely be sought for in human individuality; we

must look for it with equal earnestness in human sociality."[11] Notions of a Godhead who is social, connected, and in relation create the basis for human interaction that echoes this relationality. The trusting relationship that the triune God has within Godself becomes the foundation for the social interaction between followers of that God. Divine trust becomes the model for human trust.

Church historian Martin Marty furthers this argument, making a connection between transcendence and imminence in trust.[12] He suggests that *divine trust* and *human trust* are not the same but analogical: "God alone can be trusted absolutely," but "when we use the mirror of divine trust on the human scene, some similarities, metaphors, examples, and mandates for consequent action can inform human trust."[13] In other words, trusting God and trusting others are distinct actions but not disconnected. *The ways we trust God spill over into our experience of trust in community.* Transcendent trust begets imminent trust. Once this divinely created trust spills over into our human relationships, we begin to live into and out of that trust. Theologian Catherine Keller writes that this is crucial to the life of faith: "Faith is not settled belief but living process. It is the very edge and opening of life in process. To live is to step with trust into the next moment: into the unpredictable."[14] Thus, she claims, faith is imminently connected to the "risk of trust." She adds, "This 'truth' has little to do with right or wrong belief or dogma; nor is it some eternal verity engraved in our souls; it is a truth of right relation, to be embodied and enacted. This faithfulness cannot be boiled down to propositions; but it will transform our language, and indeed our propositions. Faithfulness in the genre of truth means trusty language. The true is the trusty."[15] She expounds on this theme, using several examples from the Hebrew Scriptures (including the Psalms and the creation stories), Paul's writings ("power . . . made perfect in weakness," 2 Corinthians 12:9), and the Gospels (most notably Jesus' Gethsemane prayer) to explain that the scriptural record holds fast to this idea that truth is most basically a conception of risk and trust. *Faith* is not primarily a coercive "overpowering" or "lording over," but is something else entirely.

Keller asserts that truth, theology, and indeed the very nature of God are found *in the process*. The relationality that knocks down the absolutism of the left and the right is an important antidote to the forces that threaten to divide us. It breaks down our traditional notions of power and love. Instead of overpowering from either the left or the right, the very nature of God-created power is more concerned with building up, or "empowering." She names this power as "qualitatively different" from coercive force. It is, instead, "the contagious influence that flows from a *radically vulnerable strength*."[16]

This concept suggests important theological implications for the way we view God, truth, power, and trust. Keller and others suggest that what is needed is neither absolutism nor relativism, both of which depend on overpowering violence to self, others, and community. Instead, what is needed is trust marked by *risk*, *relationality*, and *vulnerability*. These are the commitments the Godhead has eternally created, the Bible has consistently celebrated, and the church has desperately needed. If we accept Moltmann's notion of divine trust within the Godhead, Marty's conception of our trust in the divine spilling over into our trust of one another, and Keller's radical conceptions of trust understood in process, how then might the church look? What does a healthy dose of trust—especially a trust defined by interrelationality, risk, and vulnerability—bring to our congregations? In the following section, we pose questions such as these as we move toward the practical application of these theological concepts.

Polity Questions: Adaptive Church Practicalities

Who is in charge around here anyway? This polity question that began our chapter is still a relevant one. The question of authority matters. What is the expected role of the pastor and staff? As an ordained Moses, leading the way up the mountain, or as a Miriam/Aaron, serving as a supportive partner to the authority of a church moderator/lay leader or a church council? Are staff and key leaders on the same page, healthy, aware, and respectful of their roles and boundaries?

Who else is in charge around here? Again, differing polities suggest differing roles for denominational leaders who stand outside of the congregational system. Are such leaders authoritative in their pronouncements about what can happen in the congregation, or are they advisers and supporters of the decisions that congregations are free to make on their own? Or are such denominational executives nonexistent in a truly independent congregational system? As well, are there other authoritative voices outside of the congregational system: sister congregations or partner churches, or organizations devoted to a specific cause or advocacy identity that might offer support or counsel for the question at hand? Such advocacy organizations have the benefit of a history of walking through issues with multiple congregations in multiple contexts, but they often come with assumptions about what the congregation *should* decide.

Right, but who is really in charge around here? Who are the hidden leaders of the congregation? Is there a legacy member with an authoritative voice, a big donor, or a powerful cohort that calls the shots? Perhaps more importantly, are they on board with the church process or ready to torpedo it when given a chance? Family systems theorist Edwin Friedman suggests that resistance or sabotage is "part and parcel of the systemic process of leadership,"[17] and congregational leadership would do well to consider hidden voices that might be largely untrusting of leadership or the process.

Just how trusting are we? This leads us to another question that might be helpful to consider before a process begins. Regardless of denominational or historical polity, individual congregations are systems that are filled with examples of trust and distrust. While a concept like trust is difficult to measure, Robert A. Harris, a coach for pastors and church leaders, offers some key questions that might help a congregation consider their level of trust. He writes to pastors in a new call, but his questions are a helpful guide to any congregation wanting to assess how members and church leaders interact with one another, especially in the context of emotionally laden issues:

- During meetings, how do members interact with one another? Do particular members seem to distrust one another? Are there alliances (e.g., old-timers versus newcomers)?

- What signs of respect or disrespect do you observe and hear? Is there easy laughter, or are there tense interchanges?

- What issues seem to make people anxious? What do you suppose is behind the anxiety? How might you find out what is creating the anxiety? With whom might you talk?

- Ask similar questions as you observe the interactions of staff members. What is the emotional temperature of the office? Warm? Icy? Frightened? Try writing a metaphor or two describing what you experience.[18]

Just how purple are we? Related to the question above, considering the "purple-ness" of a congregation is a helpful step. Ideological and political commitments are complex, and it is dangerous to assume that just because someone has a "blue" commitment on one issue they will follow suit on other issues. Also at stake is whether a congregation identifies themselves as "purple" and what that means. Part of the reason we use the metaphor of elasticity is that it highlights a more general sense of openness to the other in all forms, not just the rigidity of absolute political camps. How does the congregation talk about and embrace these differences?

Who doesn't have a voice? Many of the cited authors in this chapter have encouraged us in different ways to think about who gets left out in congregational conversations. Who is on the margins? Who are the priests at my elbow that might need to be invited to speak and protected from reprisal? How does congregational leadership *em*power and not *over*power? Is the voice of the other heard and valued? Are any voices chilled or ignored? Who "controls the microphone" in congregational engagement? It is helpful to remember here Goleman's distinction between "high road" processes of trust, marked by cognitive awareness and reasoned clarity, and "low road," gut-level trust. Often voices might be chilled because they simply don't feel safe enough to risk vulnerability, even if they rationally accept that they have the freedom to share.

Complicating this section is the question of *who has a voice but doesn't think they do*, because they are now being asked to share power in a different way. In most congregations, there are voices who are accustomed to being listened to because they always have been, and in the presence of shared power or a differing opinion, they might feel unheard or even discounted. More to the point, if their perspective is not valued or even given the preferential treatment they are used to, they might feel like no one is listening or like their trust is betrayed.

How might congregations be intentional about hearing their concern but also encouraging them to share the microphone? Maring and Hudson, in their classic polity manual, remind us "that the Holy Spirit may speak through the humblest member. The more articulate and self-assertive members should not be allowed to monopolize the discussion to the exclusion of others. Each person must be given full opportunity to speak, and the words of each person should be carefully pondered."[19]

How will we hear the voice of God? How will we read Scripture together? What is the place of biblical authority, and how is that relevant? Is interpretive power held by a few "specialists" (i.e., trained staff or revered Bible teachers), or is there room for multiple voices speaking on God's behalf? What about other spiritual practices? Shall we regularly pray together, and what will that prayer look like? Who will lead? In some congregations, prayer and discernment are closely linked. In others, a shared mission is what builds the deepest trust. In many "the church that plays together stays together." How does the congregation talk about the work of the Holy Spirit in their midst and what role the Spirit might play in their discernment process?

What is the role of denominational polity guides, or the oft-consulted *Robert's Rules of Order*? How do we make decisions? How will we know when one has been made? Does a leader make a pronouncement? Consensus is reached? A vote is taken? If there is a vote, is there a fair way to determine the number of options available and how to choose between them?

Congregations often talk about "discerning God's will" in a matter; if this is the language used, who decides what God's will is in the current context and when it is reached? We will examine in the following chapters several real-life congregational processes, how they were created, and the advantages and disadvantages of various forms of discernment and decision-making.

What if we cannot agree? This is perhaps the most feared and often-asked question on the list. Congregations have bound themselves together for entire lifetimes, if not multiple generations. The threat of losing members or splitting a congregation hovers over every controversial conversation, with stability and comfort hanging in the balance. Yet the manner of controversial issues is that it is incredibly unlikely that the entire congregation will be satisfied by the end of that discernment. Emotional and divisive issues are emotional and divisive for a reason. If congregations waited until every single member agreed on a decision or acted out of fear that a church split might occur, our churches would be very different than they are today. Cultural change rarely happens with 100 percent consensus. What forces—seen or unseen—are at work in your congregation's social/emotional/polity system to keep the status quo? Is the change we are discussing important enough to risk the goal of "staying together"?

What about me? Again, dear reader, you have picked up this book and presumably read this far, for a reason. Perhaps you are a congregation member sensing a need for change. Maybe you are a pastor or staff person sensing a growing divide and knowing there is a need to address it. Some of you may represent an organization or denominational structure that works with many different congregations, and you hope to find ways to walk beside churches in their discernment processes.

Regardless of your role and position, it is important to ask what you bring to the table. How is God preparing you for this moment? How can you bring healing to a divisive context? How are you a priest? A prophet? How are you invested in this emotionally laden issue, and what biases do you bring to it? How many scars do you have from previous battles fought? How aware are you of your emotions and intuitions? Are you dependent on feelings more than logic, or vice versa? Over these last several pages, we have learned some new terms, concepts, and metaphors for the journey ahead. Let us continue to explore how the concept of trust can be understood and communicated in the church by examining metaphors for a trusting church.

NOTES

1. This chapter relies heavily on material from a previously unpublished thesis: Matthew B. Sturtevant, "The Red and Blue Body of Christ: Preaching Trust of God and Other in a Purple Church" (DMin thesis, Chicago Theological Seminary, 2019), 10–36.

2. Nancy T. Ammerman, Jackson W. Carroll, et al., eds. *Studying Congregations: A New Handbook* (Nashville: Abingdon, 1998), 7.

3. Daniel Goleman, *Social Intelligence: The New Science of Human Relationships,* (New York: Bantam, 2007), 16–22.

4. Goleman, 22.

5. Katherine Hawley, *Trust: A Very Short Introduction* (Oxford: Oxford University Press, 2012), 35–36.

6. Jonathan Haidt, *The Righteous Mind: Why Good People Are Divided by Politics and Religion* (New York: Vintage Books, 2013), 53–59.

7. Haidt, 54.

8. Haidt, xx.

9. Haidt, 343–61.

10. Haidt, 371.

11. Jürgen Moltmann, *The Trinity and the Kingdom: The Doctrine of God* (Minneapolis: Fortress, 1993), 199.

12. Martin E. Marty, *Building Cultures of Trust* (Grand Rapids: Eerdmans, 2010), 49.

13. Marty, 50.

14. Catherine Keller, *On the Mystery: Discerning Divinity in Process* (Minneapolis: Fortress, 2008), xii.

15. Keller, 36.

16. Keller, 90, emphasis added.

17. Edwin H. Friedman, *A Failure of Nerve: Leadership in the Age of the Quick Fix* (New York: Seabury Books, 2007), 11.

18. Robert A. Harris, *Entering Wonderland: A Toolkit for Pastors New to a Church* (Lanham, MD: Rowman & Littlefield, 2014), 34–35.

19. Norman H. Maring and Winthrop S. Hudson, *A Baptist Manual of Polity and Practice*, rev. ed. (Valley Forge, PA: Judson, 1991), 62.

3

Metaphors for an Elastic Church

Do you relate to this scenario? Pastor Helen opened her inbox with typical anticipation. Would today's email bring comments about her sermon or what her outfit looked like? Would she face another complaint about the ushers taking up the offering in shorts? Not this time. This time she was floored by a first-time visitor's question. The visitor seemed excited to be there and ready to return. "My partner and I are new to town and wonder if we would be welcome at your church. What is your policy on welcoming LGBTQ persons?" Pastor Helen didn't have a good answer. She stammered through a recitation of the church mission statement without giving a clear response. After all, the congregation wasn't clear about this, so how could she be? The rest of the day, Pastor Helen wished she had a better way to respond.

Clarity around such questions is essential to the health and well-being of a faith community. The journey to clarity requires a willingness to stretch out of familiar comfort zones. Such a stretching as a church can be described as an *elasticized ecclesiology*.

An Elasticized Ecclesiology

Philosophers and anthropologists talk about the concept of "other" and "otherness" in technical terms. The word *alterity*, in a broad sense, is the awareness of individuals, communities, and perspectives that are different from ours. The process of *othering* is often aggressive or even violent: marginalizing, oppressing, or even physically imprisoning (or worse) those unlike us. Ulrich Schmiedel reframes this concept to speak to the church. Like many others, he bemoans what he calls both a "crisis in the churches" and "churches in crisis."[1] Waning cultural influence and shrinking participation in congregations have been a source of deep anxiety. In reaction to that anxiety, congregations often double down on their identity and distinctiveness. Many churches respond in fear by demonizing or marginalizing the other, those who somehow stand outside of that perceived identity. The unspoken (or even spoken) message is "*We* are *us*," and "*They* are not *us*."

Schmiedel hopes to turn that destructive process of othering on its head. He suggests that we should embrace the concept of alterity within the church. We should invite otherness instead of suspecting or demonizing it, because it is crucial to the health of the church. Schmiedel invites us to a radical "openness to otherness."[2] Instead of being controlled by anxious insecurities, settling into defensive positions and looking for enemies around every corner, congregations would do well to open their eyes to those who are different, choosing to listen and learn from others' experiences. Alterity should be embraced, celebrated, and made an intentional cornerstone of the local congregation and global church.

If churches learn to do this, they become what Schmiedel calls *elasticized*, choosing to grow in their perspective rather than rigidly narrowing and rejecting others outright. In other words, churches are meant to grow not only numerically but also ideologically. Instead of entering relationships with an assumption of mistrust and suspicion the way the church will survive and thrive in these times is through *radical engagement, openness*, and *trust* in the other. Churches that narrow themselves ideologically become stagnant falling prey to individualism, sectarianism, and fear-driven division. In comparison, those churches that grow in alterity deepen their relationality both to God and others.

Schmiedel asks, "How can I learn how to trust the infinite other? I can learn it by trusting finite others, letting go of myself. And how can I learn how to trust finite others? I can learn it by trusting the infinite other, letting go of myself. Relationality is at the core of trust."[3] Trust of the *infinite* and trust of the *finite* are commingled, neither one prior nor more foundational than the other. He points to Matthew 25:40—"Just as you did it to one of the least of these who are members of my family, you did it to me"—suggesting that our trust of the divine is intimately connected to our trust of the other.

The healthiest Christian communities are those that increase their level of trust and ultimately their embrace of alterity. Instead of fearing others, we must *increase our experience of others' otherness.* Schmiedel offers that an "elasticized ecclesiology would not be concerned with the preservation of identity but with the preservation of alterity."[4] The result benefits not only the welcomed other but also the welcoming church. When we risk vulnerability in this way, we find ourselves ultimately able to trust God more fully *because of* our practice of trusting others. A church focused on trust of the other grows in spiritual health, congregational health, systemic functioning, and sometimes even increased participation. As diversity grows, the community often grows numerically. A church open to alterity learns to attend to what new things God is doing in the world. The energy spent by a congregation determining what ethical, moral, or ideological litmus tests must be passed would be better spent inviting, welcoming, understanding, and growing with the other. Trust-building transforms us and our relationships.

The Elastic Church

The concepts of elasticized ecclesiology form the central core of our healthy church metaphor—the *elastic church*. Like an elastic band, meant to stretch and grow, the elastic church embraces its alterity. What if a congregation sees the value of stretching and growing in ideological terms? Instead of viewing the world and culture around them as encroaching on godlessness, might congregations begin with a curiosity about the experiences that others might bring? The elastic church invites and empowers marginalized or previously unheard voices to the table. Church, then, becomes less like a mighty fortress keeping the outsiders at bay and more like an elastic material that can accommodate new things that increases its size. Is the healthiest church the one that grows by being more elastic, stretching and adapting along with its participants—old and new?

Perhaps that is what the church has always been when at its best. This concept of an elasticized ecclesiology is closer to the original vision of the church than the bifurcated rigidity that we have seen it become. New Testament scholar at Samuel DeWitt Proctor School of Theology, Yung Suk Kim, attributes a similar message of alterity to Paul and his metaphor of the body of Christ, especially in his Corinthian letters.[5] Like Schmiedel, Kim suggests that the church ought to emphasize diversity over unity.

Messages of unity often have a colonizing effect on the church community, as well as a chilling effect on hospitality offered to those on the margins. Often those who speak of unity are liable to use their power to simply require all others to fall in line. In comparison, Kim sees Paul's metaphor of the body as inclusive and holistic, as opposed to an exclusive, "boundary-protecting" model.[6] He views Paul's language of "Christ crucified" as a message to the weak and marginalized of the world, inviting them to a radical association with Christ, who was marginalized and weak like them. Thus, for us to practice the body of Christ as Paul suggested, we are to center our community on the inclusion of diversity.

Specifically, Kim suggests the practical discipline of dialogue with others, with an intentional inclusion of marginalized voices: "Paul offers a vision of living in diversity, respecting differences, engaging the other with a self-critical awareness, and caring for the other in solidarity and for creation in wonder."[7] So Kim illumines the Scriptures in a way that suggests that this commitment to diversity and an elasticized ecclesiology has its roots in the early church and the teachings of its first major theologian. This awakening to otherness is the key to how we might respond to a bifurcated church. If we practice Christ-transforming community in the way Schmiedel and Kim see it, it suddenly becomes less important to assert that our side is right. In fact, if the practices of trust-building, welcoming, and including become the way we see God most fully, then it becomes crucial to the nature of the church that we enact trust in this way. Being the church Paul envisioned requires stretching and growing, embracing alterity, and allowing for diversity of thought and personhood.

Of course, such diversity requires thoughtfulness and healthy boundary-keeping. Must the elastic church trust equally all ideas and all propositions? Should the motto of an adaptive, growing church be "Anything goes"? Surely there are boundaries to trust: we don't hand over the keys to the church safe to a first-time visitor; nor do we put a newcomer in charge of the children's ministry. *Trust must be earned.* Inherent in Keller's process model of a "trusty truth" is a flow toward greater truth that allows for setting aside some ideas and behavior as unhealthy or problematic. Trust doesn't follow the "anything goes" path of relativism.

How then might an informed congregation keep healthy boundaries and yet reach out to those on the margins? Theology professors Grace Ji-Sun Kim and Susan Shaw write that the concepts of intersectional theology provide a path. Intersectional theology is necessary to address the social reality of changes—moving away from patriarchy, racism, biblical literalism, and gender binary complementarity:

> *In other words, intersectionality is a lens for understanding how gender, race, social class, sexual identity, and other forms of difference work concurrently to shape people and social institutions with multiple relationships of power. It is kaleidoscopic, constantly rendering shifting patterns of power visible. It is confluent, a*

juncture point where identities, locations, institutions, and power flow together creating something new. It is a praxis—an ongoing theory with activism toward social justice on the ground so that theory informs practice and practice informs theory.[8]

This enlightened understanding embraces differences among persons as it acknowledges alterity, multiplicity, and hybridity. Intersectional theology, which is covered in chapter 5, helps churches imagine and create new paths to equity and justice as it scrutinizes how power is deployed throughout the church system as well as the broader community.

Elastic Priests

Many churches representing Ammerman's congregational form cringe when they hear the word *priest*. "Priests? We don't have priests! We threw them out with the Reformation! Who needs priests when we have the Bible?"

Of course, the original Reformers were not quite so dismissive. They viewed every member of a congregation as a priest, an idea examined in Carlyle Marney's book *Priests to Each Other*, "*Priest at my elbow is of the essence! We are priests to each other.* I do not priest me. I priest *you* and vice versa. On this the community of witness takes its rise. Without it no church exists at all" (emphasis original).[9] It is a quaint but powerful image. Instead of a priest separated by distance or title, we share the priesthood with those "at our elbows." Side by side, we serve, valuing alterity and trust.

If this was radical to the Reformers or even in Marney's era, it is just as radical today. In a sense, as many issues divided the church five hundred years ago as today. Yet our division seems more profound than it has ever been. What is the difference? Perhaps if Marney were still preaching in his church today, he might point to the fact that we have failed to "priest" each other. He might bemoan our growing distrust of all authority, suspicion of those who are not like us, and a deepening search for ideological homogeneity. Marney acknowledged that this "priest at my elbow" practice is not easy, because it means that an alterity-driven gospel must "get under the feathers of our protecting images, and this is always a risk."[10] Thus, risk is inherent to our shared priesthood.

Marney also called to those in power to voluntarily lay down their privilege and share with others in egalitarian alterity. He wrote, "the gospel has meant the release of the captive, not the binding of a prisoner! . . . Sometimes the nerve to submit results in grace, release, forgiveness, acceptance, confirmation. Not rigid behavioral absolutes, but a grace, a very grand grace."[11] Thus, for those in the elastic church, this "very grand grace" invites the coming alongside others to hear their perspective—those on the margins whose voice is too rarely heard, and even those in places of privilege who somehow feel that they have been victimized. For in the hearing, vulnerability, grace, and nerve to submit, those captive to both marginalization and privilege may be released.

What if we took seriously Marney's notion that within the church there is always a "priest at our elbow"? What would it do to change the way we worship? The way we conduct church meetings? The manner in which we select our congregational leadership? How might we structure our youth and children's programming if we saw young participants as our priests? What might change in the practice of our food pantries, soup kitchens, and benevolence fund ministries if we stopped seeing people as recipients and ordained them into the priesthood? Is anyone feeling vulnerable yet?

Elastic Hermeneutics

A certain congregational business meeting is already a contentious one. Longtime friends and congregation members shoot worried looks across the room at each other. Emotions run high, and clearly various members are not in agreement about the issue on the table: whether they choose to prominently display a rainbow flag signifying their advocacy for LGBTQ+ persons. Before the meeting, the staff team had wondered how long it would take for someone to proclaim, "The Bible says . . ." They were all surprised when it showed up in the first five minutes!

How often have we heard regarding divisive issues, "The Bible is clear on this," as if that settles any disagreement? When someone evokes Scripture, it is often as a "sidearm," or "sidekick," or at least "on *my* side" in the argument at hand. But instead of clarifying and simplifying the issue, invoking Scripture often generates more divisiveness, as it raises the stakes and attempts to make one's opinion equivalent to the ruling of Scripture if not even the mind of God. Stephen E. Fowl and L. Gregory Jones, scholars of biblical interpretation, address this dynamic, writing that "there is no neutral or apolitical way of discussing ethics or doing interpretation."[12] In other words, a universal or unbiased reading of Scripture is nonexistent. Appealing to such a nonexistent reading simply sabotages healthy conversation and erodes trust.

They suggest that a faithful interpretive life is one that sees Scripture as an *outsider*. Instead of a commodity that can be used to bolster one's argument in a divided context, "scripture functions as an outsider for any particular Christian community when it is read 'over-against ourselves.' . . . To allow scripture to be an outsider is to recognize that this side of the kingdom our interpretations are provisional, always open to revision."[13]

When we adopt this perspective, it invites us to *an attitude of trust*—a humbler and more communal reading that is often lacking when the emotions of a divisive issue arise. Adaptive, intersectional congregations, marked by the trust of others and outsiders, are specially equipped to listen to the voices of Scripture as outsiders. No one owns Scripture, but all engaged in shared discernment turn toward the prophetic power of the biblical witness to build trust.

The willingness to hear other voices, including others' interpretations of Scripture that challenge their own, is the healthiest, most ethical way to read together. All learn together from the voice of Scripture. Instead of imagining a debate or two enemies on either side of a table, bargaining or negotiating their terms, picture those who might be on opposite sides of an ideological divide sitting together on the *same* side of the table, allowing the biblical witness across the table to inform their shared practices and change their hearts. Those who find little common ground politically eagerly anticipate that the Holy Spirit might speak through Scripture to myriad ears, filtered through myriad lives and experiences. Hand in hand, those who disagree in terms of political ideology together turn to Scripture as an opportunity to be transformed.

We will discuss more in chapter 4 about how the shared interpretation of Scripture might be engaged, especially through preaching. For now, though, we claim that the "openness to otherness" of the adaptive church applies to the otherness of the biblical witness and encourages congregations to see the power of that witness come alive in their midst.

Elastic Prophets

But must the elastic church lose its prophetic voice? Does this model lapse into false balance, marked by contrived binary terms? How far must we take Haidt's yin-yang model in the church? For every red idea, must we balance it with an "equal and opposite" blue one? For every red person in our congregation, must we recruit a blue one? Surely this is akin to Keller's relativism, the false balance of "both-side-ism." How might we avoid such contrived equality while not failing toward the dangers of our ideological silos?

Ammerman offers a helpful survey of the history of US congregations—particularly the experience of Baptist congregations—as she traces the movement of early Baptist prophets such as Roger Williams and Thomas Helwys to show how they insisted on prophetic inclusivity that was radical for their day. But as Baptists settled into a place of privilege and power in the United States by the middle of the last century, that radical edge was lost. She issues a call to return to opening our ears to those on the margins:

> *And when we discover again our responsibility to be listening for God through each other, then we will not be surprised when the message comes from what seems an unlikely source. People who are really learning to be priests together will also rediscover just how radical that message of human caring is. They will rediscover that preaching the good news means far more than securing a parking spot in heaven. . . . We are discovering again that to take seriously our role as priests is indeed a prophetic task, a task that challenges us to leave aside the old habits and listen for God's voice in new ways, through new people, leading us in new directions.*[14]

What might this look like? Adaptive and elastic priests will acknowledge that the person in the next pew might have vastly different ideas about how God is at work in the world than they have, but they can still be priests. Learning to trust all the "priests at my elbow" is difficult and complex, but it is the heart of a congregation marked by alterity. Those who become elastic church prophets choose to stand against the gleeful divisiveness of the world around us, laboring to radically welcome the others in our midst and hear their perspectives.

In a congregation divided by political or controversial issues, how might congregation members retain the power of the historical voice of the church while also learning how to hear and understand new voices? An adaptive church will learn to invite those voices and celebrate them as it shares power with those often left on the outside. Instead of fearing such differences, trusting that this is God's hope for the church gives us a new yearning to learn and speak new languages. Ammerman also suggests, "Difference is what potentially divides us, but it is also what can provide the lively energy that makes our associations truly more than the sum of their parts."[15] This is the way a healthy social system engages within and beyond its walls.

But let us remember just how complicated and radical this work quickly becomes. It is all well and good when we disagree about things that do not really matter to us or things that are relatively low stakes. But what happens when my church refuses to allow my child to be married in the sanctuary in which they grew up because of the person they chose to marry? Or what happens when my church wants to bless a union that I feel is fundamentally counter to the Scripture and the teachings of Jesus? What happens when I invite the "priest at my elbow" into this shared priesthood relationship but they have no desire for me to be their priest? With many controversial issues that divide a congregation, there are governance requirements to navigate, denominational dynamics to consider, questions of public perception and community engagement, and—whether we like to admit it—the finance committee's ever-present question of "What if we make that big giver angry and she withdraws her giving?"

Consider this scenario. Youth Sunday has always provided an opportunity for the congregation to hear from the youth. In the past, high schoolers took the congregation to task on the stodginess of the music style, the quality of coffee in the narthex, and their failure to "keep it real." But nobody was ready for what they were about to hear. The church's "Golden Boy" was about to step into the pulpit and announce that he was gay. His parents had wondered but never expected him to say it out loud, especially not this publicly. Most everyone in the youth group knew and had prayed with him as he prepared his sermon. The congregation knew to expect the unexpected for Youth Sunday, but they had no clue what was coming this year. What might your congregation do in this scenario? Would they have the elasticity to lead with trust?

Like the prophets of the Hebrew Scriptures and the prophetic gospel work of Jesus, becoming elastic church prophets is not easy. Such work raises the tension in an organization that naturally strives toward homogeneity and homeostasis. Again, Marney wrote that this *must* be the point: "The life of the church is always in an atmosphere of tension—wakefulness. Priests are a part of the surrounding tension. Tension is written into all that lives. It is everywhere. . . . There can be no moral life without tension. . . . The church, with its priests, in tension, is not the church failing. The church in tension is the church in its natural habitat."[16]

If we engage the world around the issues that matter, the injustices of our community, and the things that keep us up at night, then tension will directly result. Congregations must engage in honest, difficult, complex conversations that disrupt comfortable homeostasis but invite the disruptions of the Holy Spirit. A congregation that is dealing with tensions is a good thing, for tension is fundamental to who we are as humans. A congregation can avoid and ignore those tensions, but if it does, it is simply ignoring the tensions already present within its members. Ignoring issues does not make them go away.

To be elastic church prophets requires some stretching that might be uncomfortable but is necessary and healthy. The early church story, the human story, and the story of God's church on earth is one that necessarily lives within the tension. The DNA of the church of Jesus embraces the tension inherent to the prophetic work of faith.

Yet embracing the tension of elastic church prophets brings us to some hard truths. Prophets in Scripture and in the history of the church tend to have a tumultuous ministry and often a short lifespan. In many instances, the tension that Marney suggested that we raise is simply too much for congregation members to handle. Congregational decisions around such decisions create too much tension for some. Those who sit on the cultural divide between red and blue have often managed to do so purposefully by not tackling any issues that cause tension or division. They have held the center by not pushing too hard from either the left or right. But the nature of prophetic tension involves some pushing. Thus, some churches have made the hard decision that they cannot stay both prophetic and purple.

But with that said, we grieve the ways that many congregations choose too quickly to divide—or eject those with a certain ideology. Marney and Ammerman correctly remind us that Jesus' church must work first to be unified amid tension. Our hope is that the alterity-inviting polity that we have been exploring—together with the trust-building preaching of the next chapter and the healthy congregational processes of the chapters beyond—might maximize consensus and clear discernment and still leave room to be prophetic. Thus, we move to a final section that will help to shape some practical polity questions about how congregations might survive and even thrive through that tension.

Metaphors for Churches

Metaphorically, an elastic band, designed to stretch and grow, might be a helpful symbol for a congregation that considers itself faithful to the call of Christ. Yet this image is but one of a thousand that preachers and leaders might use to help a congregation embrace this purpose. In the following pages, we offer additional metaphors to inspire the conversation. Like all metaphors, they are imperfect. You are invited to improve, extrapolate, or contextualize them for your situation. Happy imagining!

A POINTILLIST PURPLE CHURCH
The purple church metaphor is an oldie but a goodie. Many authors have used this rather obvious image, combining the conservative red and progressive blue into a combined purple. This metaphor holds value. The simplest way to look at a purple church is to assume that each conservative becomes a little more progressive, and each progressive becomes a little more conservative until all are roughly the same moderate middle. It is akin to the model of the "melting pot" metaphor once regularly used for the United States. However, the melting pot metaphor has been largely abandoned for images of a tossed salad (each part retains its individual identity but creates a new whole).[17]

Similarly, we suggest a more sophisticated purple church metaphor inspired by the artistic world. We envision a *pointillist* purple church. The pointillism painting technique uses small dots of color painted in patterns to form an image. When viewers look closely, they see a bunch of dots; when they step back, they see something entirely different. While we are not experts in the pointillism style, we can imagine a pointillist painting that includes many red dots and many blue dots in proximity, which when viewed from a distance would look purple. This model avoids the forced homogeneity of which Kim warns. Instead, each "dot" is encouraged to be red, blue, or even their own version of purple—be who they felt called to be as a part of the larger body. Then, as they stood in with differing neighbors, sisters, brothers, and siblings in Christ, a purple hue emerged. It is not unlike a couple standing on the altar on their wedding day, preparing to light the popular unity candle. Healthy couples keep their individual identities and form something new. In the same way, a pointillist purple church recognizes the beauty of varied hues coming together to form a new work of art.

A BINARY STAR CHURCH

A second metaphor, this one from science instead of art, might be helpful as well. A binary star system is one in which two stars revolve around a common center of gravity. Each star is important to the system, and each is needed to keep the rest of the system in check. Viewed from millions of miles away, they appear to be one star. Upon closer examination, both stars are actually revolving around a single point. While there are two foci of energy, there is one center of gravity. The metaphor could be a helpful way to describe some churches. Perhaps there are two bodies—a conservative Sunday school class and a progressive small group, for instance, or maybe two identifiable leaders who have the trust of the congregation—which can account for two "ways of being Christian" in a single church. The danger with this metaphor is that it can encourage dualistic, binary ways of thinking about issues that are inevitably more complex. However, this metaphor suggests that one ideology is not "more Christian" than another, but that Christians have multiple faithful options to trust in God and one another. These two bodies form their own clusters while still recognizing that the true center of gravity is found in One who is beyond political definition. God is neither conservative nor progressive, Democrat nor Republican. Two differing viewpoints in the same church would allow people to see things differently and respect diversity.

Of course, this model requires significant work to keep different camps from becoming silos. Perhaps each identifiable leader would meet monthly with the pastor to pray for and talk about the health of the church. Perhaps these two small groups would join for monthly service projects or fellowship events. With a well-differentiated stance of the leadership, this model could encourage exciting conversation, creative ministry, and a meaningful witness to a world often unable to sustain such cooperation. Again, no metaphor is perfect, and this one would have to wrestle with the challenge of oversimplified binary thinking. We cannot be painted with such a broad brush, but when we daily live with messages of "there is only one right way to look at the world," the broadening suggestion that "there are at least two ways" might just be enough of a start.

A MIDDLE-RING CHURCH

In an article titled "The Transformation of American Community," Marc Dunkelman, who studies current political and societal norms at Brown University, describes relationships in our society using the metaphor of Saturn's rings.[18] The rings close to the planet are much like the family and friends to whom we are most closely connected. We have deep relationships and committed connections with these individuals, and we will likely make time and fully engage with them, regardless of differences of opinion or ideology. Second are the distant rings, farthest from the planet, which are much like the more distant relationships in our lives. These are loosely connected groups based mostly on one or a few common interests. We know these people only because of our single common connection—a connection that we are more likely to identify given social media capability: a shared alumni connection to a university, a common love of a certain movie or music, or a shared support of a political candidate, for example. We may belong to the same Facebook interest group as a person but not be their friend in any true emotional sense. Third are the middle rings. These are the relationships in which we will likely differ in more than one ideological issue or opinion. However, our exposure to these individuals is more than simply passing or incidental, and we cannot easily walk away from them. We find ourselves bonded to them for one reason or another. In these middle rings, we have the capability of being a community diverse enough to be exposed to differing opinions but less able to disconnect from (or to defriend on Facebook) those who offend us.

Dunkelman uses this metaphor to talk about the failings of Congress to find common ground. The middle rings at one time were the relationship practiced by political representatives, who would meet at the bars on the weekend and "work across the aisle" to find pragmatic solutions. Now those same representatives and senators go home or spend their nights Zooming with their children or grandchildren (i.e., the close rings) or isolate themselves to those constituents who are likely to agree with them anyway (i.e., the distant rings). Fewer all-night middle-ring sessions happen, and thus the effectiveness of the body is at a low point.

We believe that Dunkelman's metaphor can be instructive for the church, especially in the face of such divisive political chaos. A congregation is a network of relationships that is ideologically diverse yet also shares enough history and values of faith that the members cannot easily walk away from one another. The church has a potentially powerful role that we can play in a divided culture: we can show the world what it means to truly be purple. And as a result, we may offer a word of hope for which many in our culture search.

A SANDPAPER CONGREGATION

Those who have worked with wood know the importance of sandpaper. If a rough-hewn piece of wood needs to be shaped into a clean bowl or smooth piece of furniture, a piece of sandpaper (and sometimes an accompanying power tool!) is applied to smooth the wood. No experienced woodworker would pull out a rag to try to bring about the same result. The same is true for the difficult conversations and processes of the church of alterity. Being honest and vulnerable with each other will require some "scratchy conversations." We will need to enter an experience that is uncomfortable, uneasy, and sometimes painful. Think of the experience of the wood when it meets the power sander! Yet, for the wood to come to a place of beauty and utility, such sanding is necessary. The congregation ready to embrace alterity cannot simply sweep hard conversations under the rug but must enter into them with honesty and vulnerable hope. Sandpaper conversations are not all created equal, just as fine-grit sandpaper does not do the same work as an aggressive piece strapped to a power tool. But to assume that a soft towel will do the trick is foolish. Congregations ready to become "beautiful and useful" through the process will need to face a little sandpaper along the way.

AN AIRPLANE SEAT CHURCH

Remember Haidt's earlier image? It is helpful in the church context: sitting down next to someone on an airplane and simply talking to them and learning from them instead of assuming a posture of righteous attack. We all share the flight, so we can either pretend as though the person next to us doesn't exist, or we can make the best of a new opportunity. Likewise, riding in an airplane seat, an experience common to many, is a way of describing what our actual behavior might look like in an alterity-minded church. The airplane seat is akin to the pews in which many of our church members sit. Challenging them to engage with a bit of trust is a meaningful task. To build out the metaphor a little, a preacher might ask, "What happens if this neighbor is a parent with a screaming baby? Or someone wearing the hat of the presidential candidate you despised last election? What if this is a long transoceanic flight and you are stuck here for the long haul?" In fact, this metaphor might be a good way to remind the congregation that this will be a long flight, and it will require a return trip! The airplane-seat image acknowledges that this takes some work, but that said work is valuable to create and retain relationships in the church.

AN ELASTIC CHURCH

Here Schmiedel's notion of an elasticized ecclesiology comes into play. An elastic band is only one possible metaphor for elasticity. Like elastic, a congregation that knows the value of stretching to include the otherness of the other provides a healthy, diverse model for growth. This would be a helpful way for a congregation to welcome all beliefs, including (and especially) those on the margins. The concept of alterity would be lost on some, but many more could easily imagine the power of stretching to become stronger and more trusting of God and others. For example, a preacher could use a Pilates stretch band as a way of showing how elasticized ecclesiology grows the church like an exercise band grows muscle strength and flexibility. Alternatively, a child's slingshot could be an image of sending forth through the concept of an elasticized body; a rigid rope would be worthless on the toy, but a rubber band provides the stretch needed to propel something. The concept of elasticity is ripe for metaphorical creativity.

THE BODY OF CHRIST

Finally, the most historical and doctrinal metaphor of all: the body of Christ. This image is clearly the most crucial for congregations to embrace. Paul's metaphor can appeal to both conservatives and progressives and highlights each member as critical to the church's function. If we are to tell stories of trust to one another and build cultures of trust with one another, this biblical and practical model must be repeated and highlighted. As Kim reminds us, Paul's simple wisdom has echoed through the generations of the church, and congregations do well to remember this image as the culture around us pushes us toward specialization, bifurcation, and ideological silos. The apostle's words ring through the ages: a body of eyes alone will not do! Each voice matters, especially those voices that have historically been marginalized or ignored, and everyone's special set of gifts and personalities make the church a stronger place.

We turn now to a place where metaphors have long offered rich meaning: the pulpit. We will next consider how preaching plays an important role in building cultures of trust. The voice of the preacher is an important one in leading the body of Christ, especially in congregations that value alterity and elasticity.

NOTES

1. Ulrich Schmiedel, *Elasticized Ecclesiology: The Concept of Community after Ernst Troeltsch* (Cham, Switzerland: Palgrave Macmillan, 2017), 1.
2. Schmiedel, 22.
3. Schmiedel, 96–97.
4. Schmiedel, 271.
5. Yung Suk Kim, *Christ's Body in Corinth: The Politics of a Metaphor* (Minneapolis: Fortress, 2008).
6. Kim, 11.
7. Kim, 102.
8. Grace Ji-Sun Kim and Susan M. Shaw, *Intersectional Theology: An Introductory Guide* (Minneapolis: Fortress), 2.
9. Carlyle Marney, *Priests to Each Other*, repr. ed. (Macon, GA: Smyth and Helwys, 2001), xxi.
10. Marney, 49.
11. Marney, 60.
12. Stephen E. Fowl and L. Gregory Jones, *Reading in Communion* (Eugene, OR: Wipf and Stock, 1998), 21.
13. Fowl and Jones, 112.
14. Nancy T. Ammerman, "Priests and Prophets," in *Proclaiming the Baptist Vision: The Priesthood of All Believers*, ed. Walter B. Shurden (Macon, GA: Smyth & Helwys, 1993), 61–62.
15. Nancy T. Ammerman, "Congregation and Association: Rethinking Baptist Distinctives for a New Century," in *Baptists in the Balance: The Tension between Freedom and Responsibility*, ed. Everett C. Goodwin (Valley Forge, PA: Judson, 1997), 263.
16. Marney, *Priests to Each Other*, 65, 67.
17. James L. Evans, "America as Melting Pot? We're Really More of a Tossed Salad," Good Faith Media, June 26, 2009, https://goodfaithmedia.org/america-as-melting-pot-were-really-more-of-a-tossed-salad-cms-14446/.
18. Marc Dunkelman, "The Transformation of American Community," *National Affairs*, Summer 2011.

4

Preaching: Evoking Trust through Dialogue[1]

What does trust have to do with preaching? Plenty! Preachers have long understood that trust is critical to the preaching event. If distrust occurs between a preacher and hearer, the effect is almost instantaneous: a distrusting hearer might wince at a certain word or turn of phrase, or shut down even as soon as the preacher stands to speak. In response, the distrusting preacher sees the reaction and stiffens, changing the way he or she preaches. In some cases, a lack of trust causes a hearer to walk out in the middle of a sermon. As a result of these unspoken sentiments of distrust—a stiffened reaction and less vulnerable tone—the trust level of other hearers suffers. In contrast, a trusting context allows preachers to be honest and vulnerable in the pulpit before a trusting sea of hearers. The way the preacher preaches in the pulpit matters, and so does the continuing relationship the preacher has with the hearers.

Both the sermon and the preacher are touch points of trust. Does the preacher trust the hearers enough to be honest and vulnerable? Do the hearers trust the preacher and believe that the preacher trusts God? Are there specific ways the preacher can increase trust from the pulpit? Should the preacher be explicit about naming "trust" as a shared value of faith, and what would that sound like? How is the process of sermon crafting a work of trust? Martin Marty helps us begin to answer these questions and more in his work Building Cultures of Trust.[2]

While not only addressing preaching, he offers principles that are imminently applicable. He suggests seven levels where "risk and trust meet."[3] We focus on four as we explore the preaching event and congregational relationship in the building of trust. First, we survey the context of the congregational community, including how the relational connection with the preacher builds the sermon and creates trust. Second, we examine the power of stories, or as Marty names it, the place "where stories get told or heard." The power of narrative cannot be overstated. We will then move to more traditional homiletical categories: first to content, or "where teaching trust may occur," asking if there are times and ways that preachers can specifically teach about trust, explicitly and intentionally. We conclude with form, referencing what Marty names as "places of intermediation," considering if there are certain ways to structure the sermon to evoke trust.

Trust-Building in Community: Trust Is Earned

Trust originates in relationships. As the preacher stands in the pulpit, the words the listeners hear are in the context of relationship. Most hearers know the preacher, and depending on the church, the preacher often knows most of them. The preacher and listeners have a relationship—often one marked by trust. Marty recognizes that building cultures of trust requires earning that trust through relationship and conversation: "Conversation furthers education, helps entertain, builds social circles, and is a scene where participants can seek to build trust."[4]

All that sounds good until the preacher starts talking about abortion! Community and trust often go out the window after the sermon on same-sex marriage, gun control, or any other of a host of ideological issues that tend to create a wedge between us. Jonathan Haidt, the social psychologist who explained how our trust is based on both cognitive and intuitive connections, suggests that religion both "binds and blinds."[5] It binds us together in ideological partnerships and blinds us to the moral commitments of those who are not in our ideological network: "We think the other side is blind to truth, reason, science, and common sense, but in fact, everyone goes blind when talking about their sacred objects."[6] While not a homiletician, Haidt's concepts are helpful for preachers wondering how they can preach to someone within their community who is not within their ideological worldview. How might conservative preachers reach the progressives in their congregations, or how might progressives reach the conservatives? How might trust be built when so many intuitive and cognitive processes blind us to the perspectives of others? Haidt's suggestion is akin to his airplane seat metaphor: "If you really want to open your mind, open your heart first. If you can have at least one friendly interaction with a member of the 'other' group, you'll find it far easier to listen to what they're saying, and maybe even see a controversial issue in a new light."[7] While not knowing the brain science behind it, the seasoned preacher knows this truth all too well: before hearers will trust a preacher from the pulpit (especially one who preaches in tension with their worldviews), they have to open their hearts to that preacher. Likewise, before the preacher can connect to hearers, the preacher must open his or her heart to them. Then and only then will both conservatives and progressives start to open their minds to hear, understand, and trust, engaging one another as an adaptive, elastic church.

But how will we as preachers know what every hearer is feeling and thinking in a given moment or during a given sermon? Obviously, we cannot know with complete certainty, but O. Wesley Allen has some suggestions for intentional and thoughtful communal conversation around the sermon event. He writes that preaching must be a shared task, what he refers to as a "homiletic of all believers," a variation of the Protestant tenet "priesthood of all believers." Allen argues that the logical conception of this tenet is to trust the congregation itself to engage in the homiletic process: "If everyone is proclaiming, then the emphasis in a theology of proclamation shifts from a monological funnel (from Christ through the Bible through the preacher to the congregation and to the world) to a conversational ecclesiology in which the gospel moves back and forth among the gathered community in the form of statements and questions and in the form of yes and no."[8]

Preachers may do this in a host of ways: coffee hour sermon feedback groups on Sunday afternoons, sermon text Bible studies with congregation members or other clergy, or thoughtful conversations with church members or staff throughout the week that invite them to join the homiletic work of the preacher. Meanwhile, daily, unintentional, integrated conversations of the congregation are what feed this process. Allen suggests that "for any ecclesial conversation to be an authentic expression of the church's call to be the body of Christ, therefore, a certain amount of *trust* is necessary. The level of trust, of course, deepens as partners sustain a conversational relationship over time" (emphasis original).[9] The work of the sermon takes place in a tableau of relationships and conversations, even when preaching or the exegetical work of the sermon is not the explicit goal. Pastoral visits, coffee conversations, committee meetings, email discussions, and for many churches, "the back door" as people leave the sanctuary can be just as valuable in the work to create and build trust. For this conversation—listening to truly engender trust—Allen suggests that

> *the listening that is called for is not that of a passive, distant, unaffected observer, who overhears a conversation in order to cull materials to use as illustrations in a sermon. Nor is this an over-and-above listening like that of a schoolteacher who listens as students struggle with knowledge that the teacher could easily dispense but who withholds for the sake of the learning process of the children. Rather the preacher practices reciprocal listening; it is risky, open-minded, willing-and-wanting-to-be-converted listening.*[10]

Out of this tableau of trust comes a very different kind of preaching. Instead of a preacher who has been sequestered from her or his congregation all week magically appearing on a Sunday morning with answers from on high, a conversational preacher preaches not only to community and in community, but also from community. An elasticized preacher has been learning all week from and beside those to whom she or he now returns, offering a word. Columbia Theological Seminary homiletician Lucy Atkinson Rose[11] mentions a similar concept, referring to a style of conversational preaching that offers "tentative interpretations," "proposals," and "wagers." Preaching best comes from a place that trusts hearers, even when they are ideologically different or even polar opposites. Instead of arrogantly proclaiming one version of the truth as absolute, preachers evoke trust and curiosity with their words. Preachers ought to humbly and vulnerably share themselves in the sermon, aware that they are speaking for themselves and not on behalf of some perfect, disembodied truth. Preaching must embody an ecclesial community, an absence of hierarchy, the little truths of personal experience, inclusiveness, and a conversation with Scripture. It must come from a place of trust of other—both within the congregation and outside of it—and that must be seen in the pulpit: "Always at the heart of conversational preaching is the experience of connectedness, the sense of community and mutual independence, of trust and safety, that allows all participants to speak out of their personal experiences, interpretations, and wagers."[12]

This model of preaching is not haphazard or unintentional. There are ways to plan and prepare for these conversational relationships. The ACTS (Association of Chicago Theological Schools) Doctor of Ministry in Preaching Program, a longstanding collaboration between various theological institutions in Chicago, offers one model. They require students to create a Parish Project Group (PPG), a covenant group of congregation members who agree to meet with the preacher before and after each of several sermons throughout the academic year. At the meeting prior to the sermon, the group discusses the text and direction of the sermon. Then they meet again and offer feedback and evaluation. The PPG is rooted in the congregation itself and has the goal of building trust between the hearer and the preacher. Allen suggests that this is exactly the process needed to build trust within the community. It is a meaningful example of what he calls "conversational ecclesiology."[13] The PPG allows congregations to engage in a three-year covenant group that builds and sustains that trust through conversational relationships. It helps the preacher to be clear with expectations, listen to the variety of input from the group, use their input wisely and confidentially (unless permission was granted) in the sermons, and offer thanks for their support. One of the results of this process is that the congregation and preacher each engage in the risky work of trust.

During my (Matt's) preaching experience with this program and group of lay leaders, I found the model to be incredibly helpful to trust-building and learning. During my studies, our congregation considered that if this process would work a few times a year with a small group of selected individuals, could it work on a more regular basis? We used the PPG model to create a similar dynamic on a more consistent basis. On Wednesday nights before the COVID-19 pandemic, and then shifting to Zoom on Sundays, we have held what we call the Two-Way. Based on the PPG cycle of shared exegesis/shared evaluation, we combined the two experiences each week for a session of both feedback (of the previous week's sermon) and Bible study (of the coming week's text). Before the pandemic, participants met in person, but they continued to meet regularly via Zoom when they became separated physically. The number of participants dipped, but the conversation was not any less lively! Coming out of the pandemic, we continue to meet both virtually and physically, inviting any and all members of the congregation to participate every week. Like the PPG, the goal of the Two-Way is to participate in Allen's "conversational ecclesiology." Participants in the process are often surprised at their ability to collaborate in the sermon, and we have found it to be an indispensable time to test ideas, hear new perspectives, and understand better how sermons are heard. It is a practice of building deepening trust over time through conversational relationships. All involved have been thankful for the trust built through their work. The shared homiletic process intentionally invites voices to participate in the work of the pulpit. While most of them never step onto the chancel, they are deeply involved in the work of the sermon. As a real-time iteration of Schmiedel's "elasticized ecclesiology," the goal is to increase participation, invite engagement, and grow in diversity of thought and perspective.

While this concept and practice might be helpful in many churches, other preachers might ask, "Why wait until after the sermon?" The practice of "call-and-response" preaching creates a similar dynamic during the preaching event. Frank A. Thomas, homiletician at Christian Theological Seminary in Indianapolis, suggests in his *Introduction to the Practice of African American Preaching* that call-and-response "refers to the interaction between preachers and congregations all over Black America that allows the audience to partner in shaping and directing the sermon. Based on oral traditions in west and central Africa, the preacher says something, and the congregation says something back. The preacher often makes a sermonic plan in the study, but feedback from the audience often leads to improvisations initially unforeseen by the preacher."[14] In the same way that coffee hours, "backdoor" conversations, and Two-Way type programs provide feedback and trust-building over the course of a week, in call-and-response churches, the feedback process is nearly instantaneous. Feedback is asked for and received. Pushback or disagreement is obvious. Support and encouragement are vocalized in profound ways. In some sense, this style is a distilled version of the same process that Allen names above. The sermon is created and shared in community, a true "homiletic of all believers." When controversial issues are broached in the sermon, preachers must read the verbal and nonverbal cues in the moment, adjust on the fly, and remain faithful to both the initial aims of the sermon and the congregation's immediate response. For those preaching in the call-and-response style, the ongoing challenge is to understand the congregation's shared homiletic practice and build trust throughout the community in the preaching event and beyond.

The elastic church comes in all shapes and sizes, with a multitude of preaching expectations and styles. Whether a congregation of "frozen chosen" hearers is silent in the pews and needs organized prompting to share feedback, or a group of verbally engaged hearers shares that feedback freely and boisterously in the sermonic event itself, adaptive preachers have space to build trust, demonstrate openness to alterity, and create community. This process takes place before, during, and after the sermon. They can address difficult topics, introduce controversial issues, and even speak hard words because trust and relationships exist both within and beyond the sermonic event. As preachers create a homiletic of all believers along with their hearers, the blinding is lessened and the binding is intensified. Sometimes the words that are spoken are less important than the relationship that stands behind those words.

Trust-Building through Story:
Trust Is Imagined and Told

Yet the words do matter! Building cultures of trust requires close attention to words and how they are shared. Marty refers to a second trust-building element as the place "where stories get told and heard."[15] Preaching has long had a narrative aspect. Ancient religious texts used stories to convey meaning and profound truth. Jesus used parables consistently to share his message. Stories create cultures of trust. Communities tell stories to one another, and such stories can be tools for either trust or distrust. The Bible is a collection of stories about trust: how and who to trust, and what happens when we trust wisely (or unwisely). The ways we tell stories to one another, frame truth to one another, and vulnerably share our understanding of ourselves all contribute to the work of trust.

Scholar of law and theology at Boston College, Cathleen Kaveny[16] describes a storytelling method that simultaneously makes sharp and salient points about the current context while also removing some of the vitriol and anger endemic to the jeremiads of many contemporary preachers. What she calls "prophecy without contempt" utilizes humor, irony, and winsome narrative to invite—rather than drag—the hearer into hard but important topics. In a context that is immediately distrusting of anything that feels "political" or attacks issues head-on, story can allow for truth-telling that beckons instead of confronts. Preaching stories is a meaningful way to evoke trust, include the marginalized, and be prophetic while still trusting one's hearers. Kaveny highlights the book of Jonah, which tackles hard concepts such as nationalism, racism, and institutional violence, but does so in narrative form. A fish, a vine, and a prophet constantly tripping over himself give the reader a laugh, all the while being used to tackle hard topics. Consider a portion of a contemporary sermon delivered during a tense and anxious time within a congregation and the country. In November 2018, Matt preached the "Grandma's House" sermon series hoping to acknowledge the tension present between hearers and preacher but not ratchet up the anxiety already present in the room.

> *The family worship service had been the family [Thanksgiving] tradition at Grandma's house for as long as grandson Zach could remember. By Wednesday night, everyone had arrived from work or from flights, found something for dinner in the fridge, and tried their best to pick off a piece of the smoked turkey without Grandma swatting their hand away. After the football had been tossed in the yard and the last trip made to the grocery store before it closed for the holiday, everyone sat down in the living room. Aunt Patty sat down at the piano. Grandma had borrowed hymnals from her Baptist church, and while she was out retrieving the books, Zach reminded the newbies of the rules:*
>
> • *One, Grandma is in charge. She has worked hard on this, and this is really important to her.*

- *Two, everyone participates. This is not an optional event. You don't have to have a perfect voice to sing or perfect attendance in Sunday school. Everyone participates.*

- *And three. No Christmas songs. Don't even ask. Not a "fa, la, la" or a "jingle bell" or a "holy night" will be uttered in this house until the day after Thanksgiving. No exceptions. As Grandma says, "We are thankful together. Then we wait for the Christ child together. End of story."*

So, they sang the thanksgiving songs: "Count Your Blessings," "We Gather Together," and "Come, Ye Thankful People, Come." Everyone in turn said something they were thankful for this season. It had been a hard year for some, so that part was particularly meaningful. Then Grandma stood up to read Psalm 146.

Zach couldn't help himself. It just slipped out. He had been on the leadership of the Christian Democrats Club at college and had been rather full of anger and anxiety the last few months—and rather full of himself after Election Day when his state candidate won. He had not said a thing the whole afternoon and into the evening. But he could not hold on any longer. He couldn't help himself: "Don't put your trust in princes, huh? It would be nice if our 'prince' in the White House would read this."

And in an instant, everything fell apart.

His uncle Jeff, who had proudly worn his Make America Great Again hat to the dinner table, itching for a fight, pounced: "What is that supposed to mean? It's nice that we finally have someone in the White House that doesn't hate Christians! Finally, there is someone in there who we are able to trust! I don't know what they are teaching you at that school, but it is high time that someone let you know the way the real world works."

Other family members began to jump in, and the conversation degenerated further from there. Zach and Jeff were up

*out of their chairs, screaming at the top of their lungs; Zach
had grabbed Uncle Jeff's MAGA hat and was threatening to
throw it into the fireplace. The granddaughters waved their
arms as they tried to make their points heard. Both of their
husbands were sitting in stunned silence, trying to figure
out what had just happened. The great-grandchildren were
standing in a corner crying. Grandma's worship service had
become something between a political debate and a WWE
cage match.*

"Stop!"

*Grandma's voice was louder than any of them had ever
heard. "We will not do this here. We will not do this now.
There is a time and a place for debate. But it is not during a
service of worship of God in my home. If you all had listened
long enough, I had some things that I wanted to say about this
psalm. I have been working on it for a month. Now, I kindly
ask you to return to your seats and listen to what I have to
say." The silence was immediate. Everyone did exactly what
they were told, sheepishly returning to their seats, their faces as
red as the cranberry salad in the fridge.*

Using familiar themes of Thanksgiving dinner, generation
gaps, and "Grandma's house," interspersed with all too familiar
contemporary political disagreements, this example of preaching story invites us to laugh at ourselves. Instead of confront-
ing issues head-on and setting up an "us versus them" dynamic,
a narrative format can offset the tension and help hearers create what Kaveny calls "empathy with one's opponents."[17] This
homiletic model can be crucial in our current context of verbal
war, becoming a hopeful and restorative word that is both firm
on its principles and humble in its delivery. This approach is not
a perfect solution and carries with its subtlety the risk of being misunderstood. However, when tension is high and the trust
relationship is on rocky terms, narrative characters can benefi-
cially stand in the place of direct confrontation between church
members or between hearer and preacher.

Sometimes the story that will engender the deepest trust is our own. When the preacher shares their own story honestly and vulnerably, they might earn the deepest measure of trust from hearers. Explaining their own story, how they came to a certain ideological commitment through experience or even pain, carries with it an invitation to relationship. Be warned, however: such vulnerability from the pulpit clearly bears risk. Our own stories, especially those of pain, are holy gifts to share with others, and it is possible that the time or place is not right for such sharing. Consider wisely the sharing of such a gift and what cost it carries. If the trust relationship between preacher and hearers is unhealthy, such a gift can be abused. But for those ready to engage in such vulnerability, in an emotional state healthy enough to share, and surrounded by supporters within and beyond the church, the sharing of our stories can be a beautiful opportunity both to show and invite trust.

Trust-Building as Content: Trust Is Taught

A third category from Marty is "where teaching trust may occur."[18] For a congregation to move together through controversy, there are appropriate times to name trust as a shared value. If a congregation is to be a trusting, alterity-minded church, they must learn to embrace the tasks of trust and openness to otherness. In short, they must feel called to this way of being church. Doing church in this way is indeed possible, but it seems that the congregation must be emotionally capable and willing to commit to the vision of being an "elastic church." They must be as committed to this idea of an elasticized ecclesiology as they are to their own political and ideological commitments. Congregation members must be strong in their own beliefs and ideology while committing to the idea that they are sometimes better off alongside those who do not share that ideology. In short, for an elastic, adaptive church to work, the congregation must see themselves as such and accept that task and identity. A level of self-examination and self-identification must be present for congregation members to be willing to say, in essence, "I don't want to be around only people who are all like me. I want to be in a church in which we know we are different and we appreciate and value those differences." This can be a value of conservatives or of progressives, but it is not a presumption of either. Congregants and staff must not only be able to trust God and the other, but they must hold an inherent trust in the value of a congregational commitment to alterity.

Therefore, to succeed in this crucial type of church, its leadership—including the preacher—must be able to teach trust as content, using a multitude of tools, intellectual and emotional. To accomplish this goal, preachers must preach to the whole person. Goleman and Haidt teach us that the trusting brain must make connections emotionally as well as intellectually. Frank Thomas echoes their perspective, inviting the preacher to be intentional about these multiple layers of trust-building: "The cognitive is the faculty of reason and rational thought. The emotive is the base for the arousal of feelings and affections. The intuitive is the capacity for direct knowing or learning beyond the conscious use of reasoning."[19] Preachers must open the toolbox and use a full complement of options. At times scriptural and theological conceptions of trust must be explicitly named. Perhaps the preacher calls upon one of the theological voices from this book or elsewhere to describe trust in an intellectual or cognitive way. Maybe the preacher calls upon a metaphor, like the rings of Saturn or the pointillist purple church suggested in chapter 3, to make such conceptions more comprehensible or memorable—cognitive content that offers profound theological ideas about trust, offering an alternative to something they assumed before the sermon, or perhaps rational evidence for an idea they already believed. Meanwhile, sometimes an emotional call from the pulpit helps hearers to tap into their joy, sadness, empathy, anger, or a host of other feelings. Or maybe it is a story that best weaves together the intellectual and emotional teaching of trust. Preaching to the whole person offers a multiplicity of content.

What we actually say about trust matters. In the previous pages, you will find plenty of trust content. The theologians, ideas, stories, and metaphors might be a good starting point for your own sermon on trust, or they might inspire you to find content that is more relevant to your congregation. But now that we have a collection of content about teaching trust, what do we do with it?

Trust in Form: Trust Is Crafted

When my son was younger, we loved assembling colorful plastic toy blocks together. When he received a new set, we would follow the directions (more or less) to create the vehicle or playset designed by the plastic block company's hardworking engineers. But inevitably, after months and years of play, those creations would lose pieces or break apart altogether, resulting in a large box of random pieces. But this is where the fun began! By pulling out various pieces, seeing how they might fit together in new and creative ways, and tossing aside pieces that didn't seem to fit, we found a new level of enjoyment.

This is not unlike the task of the preacher. In the preacher's mind, in a word processor file, or scribbled on random scraps of paper, the preacher has gathered various pieces of content for the sermon. A bit of commentary wisdom. A story that seems to fit. A metaphor that may or may not belong. Now the fun begins! The fourth and last of Marty's levels where "risk and trust meet" is what he calls "places of intermediation." He suggests that this work of building community and cultures of trust requires more than a happy accident. Such work requires those trained as meditators to buffer between communities and the forces that conspire to divide and splinter them. Scientists, scholars, and other professionals are called upon to use their training and gifts to intentionally engage in this practice of intermediation. What about preachers? Is there power in a trained and skilled rhetorician using intentional strategies for crafting a sermon that might mediate between these various ideologies, evoking trust and not competitive discord? In other words, is there value to how we put together the various plastic block pieces of a sermon?

Again, Frank Thomas argues effectively that this is indeed the case. He draws on the insights of African American preaching and its rhetorical style to suggest that *how* a sermon is crafted is crucial to the way a hearer comprehends and receives the message. Trained and gifted rhetoricians can craft for trust. He suggests four elements to an effective sermon: "situation, complication, resolution, and celebration."[20] Like a good sitcom or dramatic movie, the sermon that moves the hearer through these stages can create both an intellectual and emotional impact. Thomas describes an emotional/intuitive introduction that builds trust, some exposure to the "complicating" hard word of the text and the hearers' context, the gospel's response to that complication, and an emotional/intuitive celebration at the end.

How the preacher gets there, week in and week out, will look different. And of course, no one "right" way to craft a sermon exists. Each preacher develops his or her own crafting practice and favorite form over time, often starting with the familiar and adjusting to the text and context. But Thomas suggests that some intentionality to the form helps move folks from despair to hope, acknowledging both the bad news and the good news of their lives. He recognizes that the traditional language of the church is not nearly as common or comfortable as it once was, and preachers must capture the imagination of the hearer through a structure that creates an analogy from the text to their own experience. When the preacher leads the emotional process of the hearer, giving them a structure upon which to hang their fears and hopes, they become the intermediary for which Marty calls. Over time hearers learn to expect to hear both honest truth and good news, and this pattern builds trust in the preacher, in the predictability and reliability of the text, and ultimately in the faithfulness of God.

Of course, this or any form, crafted to evoke trust, must only be a starting point, as the preacher uses the theme playfully and creatively to rearrange, surprise, and adjust, given the text, the community of hearers, and the movement of the Spirit. What is most crucial to the crafting is not a one-size-fits-all formula, but a measure of intentionality, an understanding of the principles of rhetoric that takes into consideration the whole person of the hearers in our presence, and a willingness to craft for trust in God's Spirit to inspire and God's people to be faithful.

So let's dump out the plastic blocks! Using Marty's recommendations, identifying the trust-evoking elements of community, story, content, and form, below is one way we could start to piece together the various building blocks of a sermon, with the goal of building trust in the context of a divisive or controversial issue. Imagine yourself as a preacher, staring at a passage from 1 Corinthians 12 and asking yourself where trust and distrust lie in the text and in the context of your hearers. A few colorful plastic blocks to play with:

A cognitive quotation and summary of Yung Suk Kim's description of "unity" and "diversity."

An intuitive metaphor for the church and how it acts like a "tossed salad."

An intuitive/emotional metaphor about the geese you saw flying south for the winter last week.

An emotional story from your own life about how you learned to trust someone whom you were predisposed to distrust.

A cognitive quotation from Keller about "trusty truth."

An intuitive summary of the context of Paul and the Corinthians, reminding hearers of similarities between their world and the biblical world.

A cognitive quotation from your favorite commentary on 1 Corinthians.

A cognitive/emotional turn of phrase delivered in a small-group Bible study in your church (and the intuitive connection that it came from the congregation, not some unknown scholar). "Most days I think that my part in the body of Christ is to be a hair on a mole!"

A cognitive turn of phrase that came to you on your morning run: "Radical body. Radical diversity. Radical trust."

Which of the above colorful plastic blocks will you keep for your new creation? Which ones will go back in the box to be used later? In what order will you place them? How do you deliver both the bad and good news? Appendix A contains one example of how these building blocks might form a conversational sermon about trust. How would your sermon differ? What would you add, amend, or leave out? Trust is earned in community. It is imagined in story. It is taught via content and crafted via form. The work of the preacher, the community in which the preacher proclaims, and the Holy Spirit working in them both is all about trust. And now the fun begins!

From Preaching to Process

We have seen the role the preacher and sermonic event can play in the building of trust in a congregation. The elements of community, story, content, and form can all be utilized in the work of creating a culture of trust. However, there are times in the life of a congregation when the conversation gets more complicated. In the coming chapters, we will examine ways that congregations might engage in a more intentional process around a controversial issue. As helpful as preaching is to trust-building, the pulpit does not stand alone.

A congregation has much in common with secular organizations as all social change is a process that involves many different players and subsystems that make the whole system function. Personalities, positions of authority, leadership styles, and the character of each individual and family involved contribute to the process every step of the way. The following chapters provide in-depth information and guidance on how to make your church system function optimally for the right outcome for you and the rest of the congregation.

NOTES

1. This chapter relies heavily on material from a previously unpublished thesis: Matthew B. Sturtevant, "The Red and Blue Body of Christ: Preaching Trust of God and Other in a Purple Church" (DMin thesis, Chicago Theological Seminary, 2019), 50–61.

2. Martin E. Marty, *Building Cultures of Trust* (Grand Rapids: Eerdmans, 2010), 17–37.

3. Marty, 135

4. Marty, 135.

5. Jonathan Haidt, *The Righteous Mind: Why Good People Are Divided by Politics and Religion* (New York: Vintage Books, 2013), 364.

6. Haidt, 364.

7. Haidt, 364.

8. O. Wesley Allen, *The Homiletic of All Believers: A Conversational Approach to Proclamation and Preaching* (Louisville: Westminster John Knox, 2005), 18–19.

9. Allen, 25.

10. Allen, 41.

11. Lucy Atkinson Rose, *Sharing the Word: Preaching in the Roundtable Church* (Louisville: Westminster John Knox, 2000), 108.

12. Rose, 131.

13. Allen, *Homiletic of All Believers*, 25.

14. Frank A. Thomas, *Introduction to the Practice of African American Preaching* (Nashville: Abingdon, 2016), 88.

15. Marty, *Building Cultures of Trust*, 33.

16. Cathleen Kaveny, *Prophecy without Contempt: Religious Discourse in the Public Square* (Cambridge, MA: Harvard University Press, 2016).

17. Kaveny, 415.

18. Marty, *Building Cultures of Trust*, 24–26.

19. Frank A. Thomas, *They Like to Never Quit Praisin' God: The Role of Celebration in Preaching*, rev. and updated ed. (Cleveland, OH: Pilgrim, 2013), 23.

20. Thomas, 72.

5

Concepts for Congregational Help:
Trust-Building Pathways

Does this sound familiar? At the beginning of the new church budget year, the pastor at First Church is planning his continuing education options. Another preaching conference? Another retreat on the beach? What he really wishes for is a place where he can learn about *how he can talk to his congregation.* How can he help them explore a changing world? How can he retain some level of integrity and honesty as he does? He's heard a hundred courses and conferences on how to be a better preacher, but how can he be a better *communicator* when the stakes and emotions are so high?

Healthy communication is key to guiding a congregation through controversial conversations. How do we effectively bring the congregation into cocreating a missional ministry? How do we shape trust throughout these processes?

The Congregation as Cocreator for Missional Ministry

As churches have responded to contemporary reality—controversies in their communities—we have observed their patterns and processes in decision-making. Our insights have been founded on three perspectives:

Abundance: There is enough for everyone. This is neither a zero-sum nor an elimination competition.

Strengths: Each and every individual possesses great potential, as does each congregation.

Systems: Human groups function as an entity, which we call a socio-emotional, relational system.

We couple those lenses with the values of human equality, equity, diversity, and faith in grace from a caring God. We sought access to new ways of seeing those outside the routine activities of the church, which has provided a better understanding of the people inside. From the intersectional, power-sharing perspective of Christ, we learned a new, empathetic, empowering, and enabling way of understanding and interacting—a worshipful work way of doing church. This way of engaging the divine and meeting the holy enables the cocreation of a heterogeneous, pluralistic, loving group, which is open to respecting, inviting, including, and collaborating with all—even those in the margins of society. We offer insights and guidelines about the necessary actions and benchmarks for practicing that process with empathetic attending and listening, as well as reconciling trust-building activities below.

First, change is challenging and difficult for us humans as it triggers internal, emotional, visceral reactions. Fear and hate are the greatest threat and therefore the enemies of faith communities today. In the following, we continue the focus on alterity—the consideration of the importance of the experiences of the other and call into question human judgments regarding the worth of other individuals. Here we address how to respond to outsiders who may also be seeking peaceful coexistence or even collaboration in their life journey and spiritual walk.

Peaceful relationships with emotional awareness, kind empathy, graceful judgments, and astutely effective communication can transform conflicts into healthy interactions, which make for the trusting bonds of authentic relationships. However, we must emphasize that we are talking about *social change* here, and social change is always connected to our own innermost holistic health, reflection, and prayerful well-being, which involves our willingness to receive, learn, and adapt.

Churches can retain focus on conflicts and get into fights while dealing with divisive, messy, emotional moral issues. In some churches, these actions result in some choosing to transfer to a more homogeneous church that thinks and acts more like them. Yet the adaptive option remains available. The requirement for accomplishing this task of being an open, welcoming community is well summarized by author and church leader Douglas Avilesbernal:

> *When we are confident that welcoming the other will not undermine who we are, our perception of the other can begin to shift from threat to welcomed addition. . . . We have explored our particular self with the intent to clarify the solid foundation that we all have. Such solid grounding can provide the confidence needed to help an individual or group welcome those who are different. This wonderful journey can and does lead us to a place where the stranger is welcomed in expectation of becoming better together instead of fear and worry about losing home.*[1]

Yes, we must first overcome our own insecurities before we can reach out and connect with others in a constructive, enlivening, healthy manner. We must never forget that in the stereotypic eyes of the public, Christians are seen as the ones who judge, condemn, and persecute those who are not like us—and sometimes they have been right. This situation calls for great humility on our part throughout the process of building trust.

This process of adaptation to gain trust is not only about mediation or compromises. It is about human beings facing each other, sharing their true selves openly and honestly while working to attain mutual respect with a shared understanding. Conflict transformation is possible. And the emphasis is on transformation. If anyone can do transformative work, shouldn't it be the Christian church founded by Jesus and his followers? Conflicting groups may still have distinct differences of opinions—some of which may be deeply held values. But whatever the conflicts are, they can be considered with a renewed focus on working together toward the things that are most important—like equality, diversity, and equity. With the insight of hybridity and the wisdom of intersectionality, every voice can be invited, expressed, heard with empathy, comforted, and considered with compassion and willingness to share authority and power. This open-minded process of interaction enables moving forward together to meet the challenges of life in harmony—following the way of Jesus.

Rather than focusing on dichotomies and debate tactics, we focus on valuing not only the importance but also the experiences of others, those who are different and have diverse identities, narratives, and worldviews. Those others may have experienced past traumas in relationships, which continue to affect their social interactions in the present. Those traumatic experiences may even have happened in interactions where someone used authority to dominate or take advantage of others, along with other forms of mental and spiritual abuse experienced as major traumas by the victims. Those traumatizing experiences leave them majorly scarred, which significantly interferes with all future interactions that require trust.

In dealing with otherness (alterity), we examine the social dynamics in human systems in communities of faith. Most churches in North America are homogeneous—most persons present share many similarities to most others who are present. Such communities of *likeness* can easily develop an "us versus them" mentality toward outsiders. Arguments defending such a mentality may include minor offensive statements like the common "We've never done it like that before"; the bigoted "Each to their own—like belongs with like; we are all more comfortable that way"; or major social aggressions like the white supremacist "I'm not a racist, but races should not mix; it is biblical—the natural order of things." Jesus, however, taught none of that.

Jesus—a master of surprises—was the greatest leader ever in shaking up the social order and the powers that be with innovative disruptions. As Jesus taught, love God and love your neighbor as yourself (see Leviticus 19:18; Matthew 22:37-39; Mark 12:30-31; Luke 10:27; and Romans 13:9). Those may be the most succinct commandments ever. The Messiah's teachings did not lead to our segregation on Sunday mornings. Instead, our human misinterpretations of and human resistance to Jesus' teachings have caused it.

Jesus promoted trusting the higher moral authority, God, who sees injustices and cares about righteous justice in all human actions. Christ preached acting justly with compassion, charity (love), and peace. Most of Jesus' teaching on judgment was not about judging the others in our lives but was about self-awareness and personally judging oneself. We recommend the Jesus Prayer, and this short version is sufficient: "Lord Jesus Christ, have mercy on me, a sinner." Jesus, with his life example and profound teachings, told us to love God, others, and self. This deeply compassionate wisdom brings us back to each one taking care of self to be holistically healthy, not only internally but also in social interactions, as well as in relationship with the divine.

Jesus was and is the Prince of Peace. The Gospels tell us that he lived an exemplary, gracious, and peaceful life. There are two types of peace: negative and positive. Negative peace is the absence of overt tension or conflict that can be due to denial, avoidance, or repression. Positive peace is attained when collaborative human actions resolve conflicts and elicit cooperative human interaction. As Rev. Dr. Martin Luther King Jr. wisely stated, "Peace is not merely the absence of tension but it is the presence of justice."[2] Elastic churches are committed to nonviolence, reconciliation, and social justice.

Many contemporary Christian churches honor and want to emulate Jesus' peace. However, some promote a passive, negative peace attained through the perpetual consensus of the church members while isolating from diverse others. That may include traditional, unwritten social rules: the rule of consensus, accompanied by the rule of silence: "Don't rock the boat (don't question authority). Don't be a troublemaker (don't speak contrary to authority)." Such statements at least imply that no dissenting or justice advocacy opinions and, moreover, no different persons are allowed (invited, welcomed, or included). All too often that becomes a dichotomous situation (tribal social context) of "us versus them," which has little room for empathy, compassion, charity, or love. We even ask, "How much room is left for Jesus there?"

Working together with kindness to attain fairness and social justice requires sidelining secular, political ideologies to see others as not only human beings but also as beloved children of God. This is Jesus' way of caring and compassion (see the raising of Lazarus in John 11:1-44), as well as his love and graceful embrace as exemplified in some of his well-known parables (e.g., the Good Samaritan in Luke 10:25-37 and the prodigal son in Luke 15:11-32). Jesus taught that materialistic human egos need to be bridled for us to act justly toward others.

However, fairness is not always the case. Christians' judgments of others, apparently from a self-perceived superiority, are often not nice, and sometimes their expressions and interactions can be aggressive and unjust. Research has shown that homosexual Christians experience cognitive dissonance and anxiety (free-floating fears), in churches.[3] This observation explains Rev. Michael Burch's statement that churches should not expect LGBTQ+ persons to enter their building if they do not have a rainbow flag displayed prominently on their property. A flag could signify to LGBTQ+ Christians that the congregation has "a possibility of being safe."[4] Unfortunately, many churches are not intently and overtly showing signs or symbols of solidarity and are not safe. However, a supportive church can help minimize the LGBTQ+ Christian's cognitive dissonance, initial visceral displeasure, and anxiety, which can enable them to accept invitations to participate.

Another part of providing a safe, welcoming, supportive, and inclusive church is learning to use inoffensive language. Preferred terminology may seem like an ever-moving target. Back in the 1960s during the civil rights movement, people of African descent asked to be called "Black" because white people were called "white." This language shift was perceived as more respectful than outdated social terms and certainly much more acceptable than racial pejoratives. Other terms to beware of are *Mrs.*, *Missy*, and even *young lady* (we were told by a middle-aged female) for any adult woman, along with *old lady* or any other disrespectful, insulting, or discounting labels, of course. *Ms.* generally works fine in the US. Also, some LGBTQ+ persons prefer to be called gay or queer rather than homosexual. Some prefer the term *same-gender loving* over *same-sex attraction*. Overall, using the generic *LGBTQ* or *LGBTQ+* is acceptable and safe. Better yet, ask individuals what they would like to be referred to and what pronouns they use. We are told that in many university classroom introductions today, every person gives not only their name but also their pronouns. The use of the singular *they* to refer to nonbinary and gender-fluid individuals is becoming widely accepted by younger generations, rather than assigning a presumed gender with the use of *he* or *she*.

Valuing Equality

In the United States, our work to attain fairness and social justice can be associated with the Declaration of Independence, which states, "We hold these truths to be self-evident, that all men [humans] are created equal, that they are endowed by their Creator with certain unalienable Rights, that among these are Life, Liberty, and the pursuit of Happiness." The proclamation is unequivocal in the statement of worth as well as the rights of every person as it calls for liberty and justice for all. Although a political statement, it assigns the "Creator" as the source of the truth it expresses. No reference was made to social status, color, ethnicity, or sexual orientation in this document. However, the dominant language of the day implied exclusions—namely, gender and race. At those times, the white, male-dominant language was appropriate because women and Black and indigenous people of color (BIPOC) were denied equal rights—as has been nearly universally true throughout most of history up to the last half of the twentieth century (granted, much work is yet to be done on this). The more recent shift to increased gender equality was a change that some mainline Protestant churches have accommodated. However, a reading of *Invisible* by Grace Ji-Sun Kim reveals that ordained female pastors still struggle to counter the white European theology that keeps them on a discouraging uphill climb within the profession.[5]

The Declaration of Independence provides a values statement aimed at diversity, equity, and inclusion that faith communities can adopt, embrace, and use in their functional operations. If they do this, it will involve less looking for the devil externally; less finger-pointing toward and shunning of other human beings. It will open our minds, our hearts, and the doors of our churches to all others regardless of their color, creed, nationality, personal beliefs, ideology, or sexual orientation. This could include welcoming all to receive services and to participate in religious practices, including worship, prayer, repentance, Communion, reconciliation, learning/discerning, marriage, teaching, preaching, or other religious activities in faith-based communities.

Equality is an egalitarian concept that is easy to embrace but challenging to actuate. However, without accompanying behaviors of respect, affirmation, and inclusion, it is nothing more than hypocritical deception. Equality without inclusion evades justice. Equality with inclusion embraces justice. The history of faith-based communities' behavioral traditions does not indicate a high level of inclusion. The principles and guidelines herein are intended to help remedy that by facilitating trust-building relationships in communities today.

Holistic Perspective to Enhance Understanding and Relationships

Viewing life from a holistic perspective, we believe each person is connected to the divine. We humans are made of a complex of five interrelated aspects (parts): body (physical), mind (mental), social (relational), spiritual (transpersonal; nonmaterial), and community (contextual; cultural). These reductionist labels share plenty of overlap, and this holistic view of humanity includes not only individuals but also other people, and even the divine. Church leaders will do well to consider this broadened paradigm of humanity to better understand the human dynamics of their congregation.

Even when examining the individual level alone, we do well to remember that we are each more than one-dimensional beings—we are both individual and social in our focus, morals, motives, and actions. We are social beings every minute of our lives, as we cannot meet our basic needs at any point in our life without other humans. We have each drunk from wells we did not dig, been warmed by fires we did not build, and eaten food we did not obtain or prepare. We need other people and must interact with them continually. We all need each other—inside and outside the church.

Religious arguments are based on values and moral beliefs. Moral reasoning follows what Jonathan Haidt called *social intuition*. Speaking of how emotion-mind intuition functions, he said, "Intuitions come first, strategic reasoning second."[6] Recall Haidt's rider on the elephant metaphor. The rider, who represents the rational mind, is perched on top and holds the reins. The elephant represents the emotional mind. Regardless of how good the logic, foresight, and strategies of the rider are, the elephant is going to go wherever it wants. Haidt concludes, "Therefore, if you want to change someone's mind about a moral or political issue, *talk to the elephant first.* If you ask people to believe something that violates their intuitions, they will devote their efforts to finding an escape hatch—a reason to doubt your argument or conclusion. They will almost always succeed" (emphasis original).[7]

We all have feelings, emotions, and intuitions. Feelings, emotions, and intuitions are too often associated only with negatives like anger, fear, animosity, sadness, or dread. More positive feelings include compassion, peace, gratitude, joy, and trust, all of which are empowering. Also, a seemingly negative feeling like guilt can motivate the positive social behavior change that alleviates the guilt by righting the wrong that was done.

Although we each can benefit from solitude and listening to the sounds of silence, no person is a rock or an island. We all feel, think, and function our best when we are getting along with all of those in our social environment (community, peace among). One of a church congregation's goals or tasks is to facilitate not only comfortable feelings but also high-quality healthy relationships among all participants—insiders and outsiders. Our approach is not focused on orthodoxy (right thinking or beliefs). Instead, we include the human religious behaviors and moral actions of orthopraxy (right behaviors, actions), and moreover the human emotions—specifically the empathy and compassion of orthopathy (right affect, right suffering, right sacrifice). Orthopathy is being humble enough to use our ability to empathize with the other (alterity) to motivate our compassions (love) and willingness to act in their best interest, rather than solely focusing on ourselves. When we participate in orthopathy we are encountering the holy as we experience the divine.

Healing Ourselves in the Process

We envision you as an active participant in a faith group that is alive and reaching out to others in their community to not only provide the good news but also build positive, healthy, mutually beneficial human relationships. A congregation functions best as an elastic church when collaborating in building trust. Adaptive churches help participants, especially newcomers, not only experience that they belong—they are enough just as they are—but also that they give and receive compassionate feelings of connection, which enables new people to experience belonging. Doing this requires an open mind and heart along with social skills for kind, beneficial behavioral interactions. The next section provides details on the necessities for building trust. This coming together to build trust can be a transformational experience for all involved.

Consider the following story. A congregant sat in worship, listening as the organist played the introduction to "How Firm a Foundation." As the music enveloped the sanctuary, she found herself thinking: what happened to that foundation? Everywhere she turned, there was change—whenever she turned on the news, when her granddaughter told her about her new relationship, and now, when the pastor delivered the sermon. She used to know what to expect when she sat in that familiar pew in her familiar church, but now she wondered if there would ever be any end to the change in her life. How do we deal with change and help others deal with a changing world?

Much of the world has rapidly changed, which has led to postcolonial, postmodern, and increasingly diverse worldviews. Complexity and challenges abound. Our contemporary life is characterized by limitless activities. Many people hold decreased credence in status quo authorities—including those in Christian churches. Church leaders, including pastors, must not only be aware of those changes but also must deal with them directly as they actively discern God's will in the matters of all the lives of the people in their community. All need awareness of the diverse narratives and multiple, intersecting identities (hybridity) of each person they encounter. And they must have self-awareness of their own emotions as well as empathic awareness of the emotions and feelings of all others (see chapter 7 for more how-to specifics). We must heal ourselves to help others heal. This will best help us to connect, communicate, interact, and interrelate with the individuals in our community as equals in an intersectional, power-sharing, egalitarian manner.

Doing relational work is compatible not only with current congregants' welfare but also with the church's outreach to their community for connection and social justice services. Relationality requires including and embracing alterity—the other, the different—and listening to them with empathy and responding to them with compassion and the love of Jesus (orthopathy). These inclusion efforts enable and empower serving and collaborating with all as they are included in worship, prayer, music,

Communion, play, and so on. In so doing, all can join the Holy Spirit of Christ in doing mission work.

What Does a Vibrant, Elastic Church Look Like?

A healthy, adaptive church puts intent, focus, and energy into being whole and functioning to maintain a community that is open and responsive. It has space and time for developing and nurturing healthy relationships not only with the divine but also with each other. It is a place where people follow the way of Jesus Christ. A lively church is an environment that communicates acceptance—where individuals can love themselves so that they can love others. And all feel supported and like they belong. It is a social system where people can be authentic and risk being open to sharing their truth, including doubts, dislikes, and vulnerabilities. It is a group of people who know that conflicts are not dangerous but rather are an acceptable part of creativity, learning, understanding, and healing. An elastic church is a place where people are trusting and trusted, which enables them to be open to new learning and adaptation to meet the demands of their busy, complex lives.

Reviewing various churches helped us in developing a new, emotionally attuned, empathetic process of understanding and interacting, which we call the cycle of building trust, which is explained below. This is a worshipful work way of doing church; a way to engage the divine by practicing inclusion, which will enable the cocreation of a heterogeneous, pluralistic, and expanding church. Sensitive, conflictual issues, especially those dealing with emotion-laden, fundamental morals, or religious beliefs are the most emotionally volatile and therefore more problematic and riskier. When the way we perceive and believe the world to be—our reality—is challenged and seemingly contradicted, we humans become highly emotionally reactive, which is a gut-level response from our emotional mind (Haidt's elephant is in charge). That emotional intensity often is experienced and expressed as anger—an automatic self-defense mechanism. But underneath the anger, the source is fear.

Humans react more viscerally and respond faster to fear than to any other emotion. But people experiencing that fear are not always aware of its presence. Others observing people in this state will notice them becoming angry or oppositional. Fearful people may engage in self-protecting actions as they react to the perceived threat to their safety. They may carry a state of general anxiety, often with an unspecific source. In the congregational context, we return to Avilesbernal's reflection on overcoming anxiety in church outreach processes: "When we are confident that welcoming the other will not undermine who we are, our perception of the other can begin to shift from threat to welcomed addition."[8] Such perceptions are what it takes to build trusting relationships in a vibrant socio-emotional, relational system that is the living body of Christ.

The presence of anxiety in any church (or social gathering) is a given, especially when in transition or dealing with challenging change. Anxiety is a natural human response to any situation where new, unfamiliar information is present. Like all other emotions, anxiety is God-given for a purpose. Experiencing something new or different can provoke anxiety, and the heightened awareness that comes with anxiety helps us to deal with it. But where does the Christian faith fit into this process? Faith and anxiety are not absolutes—having one does not eliminate the possibility of possessing the other. God's grace redirects human nature as it offers courage and hope while facing human realities in real-world contexts.

Anxiety (or any other human emotion) exists both within an individual and as an aspect of that individual's psycho-social, socio-emotional interaction with others. Human emotions always originate from perceived social interactions, including those imagined. Therefore, the context determines the meaning for the individual experiencing the emotion. The environment is always an influence—we are constantly influencing others and being influenced by them. Our behaviors are always influenced by other people and their cultures. Understanding the social/cultural context is essential because it is the socio-emotional, relational system that determines the value and meaning of human experiences. It is all about relationships—what takes place between and among people with reciprocal interactions and reinforcement of functioning positions and roles. Age-old racial divides provide a good example.

Like Isabel Wilkerson and others, we challenge any basis for the perceived position of racial superiority or discrimination. In her book *Caste: The Origins of Our Discontents*, Wilkerson discussed human similarity and cited the work of J. Craig Venter, the geneticist who ran the Celera Genomics project that completed the human genome. Celera Genomics' research findings established that all humans are 99.9 percent the same genetically. She shared his conclusion: "Race is a social construct, not a scientific one. Human beings across time and continents are more alike than they are different. Humans create differences where God made none."[9] This is essential when we are working on achieving alliance and intersectionality with compassionate actions (see below).

The Cycle of Building Trust Model

Of course, no journey is complete without a map. Where are the best roads? What sights are there to experience? How long is that trail going into the backcountry? A picture is worth a thousand words. Below is a visual representation of some of the theological and practical ideas we have shared that function as a legend to explain the processes.

The Cycle of Building Trust Model (fig. 5.1, on page 83) is a circular, progressive process. The steps are not mutually exclusive—they often overlap with some duplication of tasks, and parts of them can all exist at the same time. Thus, the model is not linear because human relationships and interactions are complex. This cyclical model was developed to give insight into the necessary elements of the trust-building process as it proceeds with gradually increased interaction, familiarity, sharing, and affirming of interpersonal trust. The steps are a series of four general goals: humility, hospitality, relationality, and intersectionality. This process involves creating relationships in a way that is aware and responsive to all individuals' hybrid identities, as well as possible intersection of various risks or hurtful encounters with discrimination they may have experienced. The tasks of the steps may overlap or be duplicated. In this model, we see a gradual process proceeding with increased interaction, familiarity, sharing, and personal trust. Risk, courage, and honest dialogue for meaningful connections (relationality) are present during every step of the process.

The model is cyclical to illustrate that it is a continual process that requires intentional goals with integrity and astute, compassionate, sensitive, and consistent work to accomplish them. The four most basic steps of the cycle are labeled *humility*, *hospitality*, *relationality*, and *intersectionality*.

Humility requires peace within that is connected to peace with God through Christ. This humility will enable enough courage to risk vulnerability, along with the insight and social skills for entering the space of the other with safe conversing and inviting actions. It is seeing the other as an equal and being able to listen instead of telling. It requires getting the attention of the other, as attention is the new currency of the information age. After success in surpassing competing distractions for the other's attention, *hospitality* describes the next step of acting through dialogue, getting acquainted, and sharing time in activities while serving individuals, families, or groups. By doing that, we establish *relationality*, or friendship (peace between). Then we can collaborate in working together. The final step moves us toward being an *intersectional community*—fully understanding one another as whole persons and sharing authority and power for peaceful collaboration (peace among). And we are back to peace within and humility with readiness to continue the mission work. This is an ongoing process in which we welcome, wonder, worship, and work together. In doing so, we connect with our mature self, other, community, and the divine.

Figure 5.1. Cycle of Building Trust Model

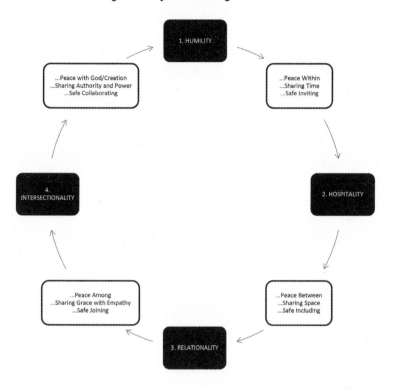

The cycle of building trust starts with humility, which is a function of peace within. Humility includes the curiosity of a growth mindset—demonstrating interest in learning from others. With that, we can be humble, caring, and willing to share our time. This requires courage and interpersonal social skills for this important, one-on-one personal interaction. We must address everyone's intuitive, emotional reactions in our communication and interaction to gain their trust at the gut level, which is different from intellectual, logical reasoning. Also, we may need to work on overcoming our own intuitive reluctance to proceed here, which is where faith, courage, and compassion come into play as motivators.

The next action step is *inviting*, which requires not only good intentions but also a willingness to take risks, which empowers that initial conversation with an unfamiliar person. If we are not intentional in setting the goal of inviting, talking to others who are different will not happen, no matter how much we say we care. Conversing is only the first part. We also must make sure that the church both is and looks like a safe place for others, even for the marginalized. We must do preparatory work with our congregations to ensure that no one offends the other, even inadvertently. Once the assurance of safety is violated, the other will perceive a betrayal of trust. Once trust is broken, it may never return to the same level. Therefore, our actions, verbal and nonverbal, must show that we care. We must be willing to strike up a conversation and listen to understand. We should overtly show empathy to provide safety for a newcomer to feel like they belong. That must be accomplished before we can share the good news of Jesus and God's grace.

If inviting has been successful, the next phase is *hospitality*—sharing our space as we begin being together in worship and in fellowship. Remember that what you see is only the tip of the personal iceberg of the whole person. We must be careful about how and what we ask of them. Safe dialogue is the way to show that we are willing to hear others' unmet needs, pain, or grief, as well as their strengths and joys. Newcomers participating in any church activity is indicative of peace between. This requires intentional actions to include the others, which is the overt proof necessary to show they belong with us church people. Sharing space can incorporate situations conducive to personal communication, like sharing a meal. While sharing the table is a symbolic descriptor for Communion, here we are talking about coffee and donuts, slushies, or even a full meal. This action step helps assure safety in trying something new, which facilitates the continued building of trust.

The practices of inviting and welcoming carry some complications. What does an invitation include? Is it inviting someone to come and be *authentic*, be their true self in the congregation? Or is it, "Come so you can learn to be more like us"? For example, some congregations include LGBTQ+ persons and say they are *welcoming and loving* toward them but have not approved of church-hosted same-sex weddings. Will LGBTQ+ persons feel affirmed by a congregation if they cannot be married in their sanctuary?

As mentioned earlier, Michael Burch recommends that churches interested in welcoming LGBTQ+ persons must seriously consider signage and symbols displayed on their property.[10] He says churches should not expect LGBTQ+ persons to enter their churches if they do not have a rainbow flag or similar signage displayed prominently on their property as symbols of safety. Yet other pastors report that LGBTQ+ persons have told them that such signage feels *less* attractive to them because they don't want to be singled out. Before placing such signage, a church must discern whether its invitation is congruent with the entire congregation's attitudes. Would LGBTQ+ persons face comments, questions, or looks in the pew, regardless of what symbol is out front? To be truly hospitable, congregations must do the hard work of discerning what their invitation looks like to those on the outside.

Once we have invited, welcomed, included, and demonstrated affirming compassion for the other—just as they are—we have arrived at the next phase—*relationality*. Sharing our mission with intentional compassion and engaging empathy enables us to come together in the work of the church. Some may call it serving. This includes providing safe opportunities for engaging in work together—inside or outside the church building. Trusting relationships built on mutual respect and collaboration solidify during this phase. Encourage new persons to join groups or take functional positions like usher, liturgist, Sunday school assistant, and so on. Acting out our faith in this way establishes peace among us and shows readiness for the process's next phase.

The final step is *intersectionality*—a word meaning we recognize and accept that individuals have multiple intersecting and overlapping social identities, indicative of the complexity of diverse life experiences. The term originates from law professor Kimberlé Crenshaw's work representing women of color at the Supreme Court and winning.[11] Professors Grace Ji-Sum Kim and Susan Shaw have drawn on intersectionality theory in their book *Intersectional Theology*.[12] Intersectional theology is necessary to address the reality of churches changing from patriarchy, racism, colonialism, biblical literalism, and gender binary complementarity. The theory calls us to recognize and accept that individuals have multiple categories of identities or identifying characteristics or hybridity. This application of the intersection concept to identity arose because much of the population has multiple identities within their personhood. For example, an individual may be female, LGBTQ+, Black, and impoverished. Characteristics like race, gender, ethnicity, religion, socioeconomic status, disability, sexuality, and physical appearance can be empowering or oppressing. All those different identifying elements intersect within a person, resulting in multiple and various ways they may be labeled, categorized by stereotypes, discriminated against, or even honored.

Intersectionality in church accepts each person as an equal— no better than, no less than any other. Furthermore, by embracing intersectionality, we become willing to share authority with those who have some differences from us—even those living in the margins—as we welcome, worship, wonder, and work together as equals. Power and accompanying privileges must be shared in a way that feels safe, good, and beneficial to the other.

The concept of intersectionality is a disruptive innovation that enables an expanded view and understanding of all aspects of the person as they truly are, the totality of their experiences— the true self. Through this understanding, we are empowered to seek truth for the sake of justice in addressing the reality of certain social situations. As we scrutinize how power is deployed throughout the church system, intersectional theology provides intellectual and spiritual ascension as it embraces and affirms differences among persons and helps church leaders create new ways toward equity to accomplish justice.

Achieving intersectionality means that your worship can include not only the celebration of the good news of the Bible but also the good news that your congregation is growing in diversity, affirmation, vitality, and power-sharing inclusion. All can feel safe and secure in trusting and joining to be regular participants or members of the church. Thus, we are back to the place of feeling shared peace, gratitude, and humility, which enables and empowers us to be strong enough to be vulnerable and take the risks of opening our hearts and talking to those who are different from us. Those actions help to share space and build trust by embracing alterity and inviting and welcoming the other.

In doing all these four phases or paths of trust-building, we invite, welcome, include, support, and affirm new people to our congregation's work in our communities. This includes those who live in the margins, those who are different, and the minorities who are lower on the power differential scale. Christians should know that in this trust-building model, prayer is a necessary practice every step of the way. With compassionate, praying hearts we can welcome, wonder, worship, and work together as we experience meeting the Holy Spirit, connecting with the divine, and fulfilling our need to connect with others. By accomplishing peace within, peace between, and peace among, we can continue this cycle perpetually for peace with God and Creation.

Honesty with kindness and a helping attitude is essential every step of the way in developing trusting relationships. I (Tim) remember what my father always told me: "A man is only as good as his word." To that axiom, I add "woman," as it is equally true for females. Empathy with sensitivity is also key for compatible relationships. This includes looking for nonverbal cues like body posture or stance and tone of voice to reveal the emotion being experienced by your neighbor. Although asking questions is necessary to get a more complete and accurate awareness of others—what they are thinking, feeling, and needing—to understand all aspects of their personhood (hybridity), it is listening with compassion that is most essential. Prayer is also required with every step to exercise our faith and enable and empower us to have the courage to act to build trust. Attending to these important aspects with every step of the trust-building process will greatly contribute to establishing trusting bonds. We can also combine these actions into the convenient acronym HELP—Honesty, Empathy, Listening, and Prayer. Table 5.1 below visually shows the process in a more linear description of the trust-building process, which includes sensitivity issues and concomitant safety concerns.

Table 5.1. The Four Phases of Building Trust: It is all about relationships.

HUMILITY
• *Sharing:* time/attention, open-mind tolerance, hope/risk, vulnerability, personal story (but only if it helps connect by showing commonality).
• *Sensitive Areas/Safety Concerns:* stereotypes/assumptions/biases, appearance of exclusivity, understanding/listening, diverse life experiences, past rejections, past traumas, showing acceptance.
• *Personal Actions/Work to Be Done:* HELP, intellectual ascension to overcome implicit biases, risk-taking, teaching right language to all, preparing all to welcome kindly by connecting/conversing/listening to others with compassion, courageous inviting, sensitive serving, communicating and demonstrating alliance.

HOSPITALITY
• *Sharing:* space, grace, church activities, worship, table, recreation.
• *Sensitive Areas/Safety Concerns:* emotional reactions, sensitivity, shame, cultural/belief-system conflicts, signage/displays, belonging.
• *Personal Actions/Work to Be Done:* HELP, social ascension to overcome personal aversions, sensitive decisions on signage/displays, welcoming/including, serving, two-way introductions to groups, empathetic dialogue.

RELATIONALITY
• *Sharing:* respect, faith/mission, life activities, community, service/work, Gospel (when they are ready).
• *Sensitive Areas/Safety Concerns:* mutual respect, wondering/doubts, equity/friendship/belonging, feeling secure despite personal challenges, boundaries.
• *Personal Actions/Work to Be Done:* HELP, self-disclosure for relational ascension, authenticity/wondering, affirmative serving, asking to work together, sensitive witnessing/testimony.

INTERSECTIONALITY
• *Sharing:* security, pain/joy, authority, power/roles, privileges, responsibilities.
• *Sensitive Areas/Safety Concerns:* shared understanding of whole persons' identities and past experiences of traumas, discrimination, experiences; newness of roles; breaches/betrayals of trust.
• *Personal Actions/Work to Be Done:* HELP, spiritual ascension, understanding of the whole person/life experiences with compassion, reciprocal commitments, joining/collaborating, sharing power/privilege/responsibility.

The process of trust-building is ongoing and continues to be ever-challenging. We provide more on the process's how-tos below. Chapter 7 also includes more specifics regarding social, communication skill development, and facilitation of group processes. Here we conclude this section with a suggestion for individuals and congregations: refrain from pushing orthodox theology and conversion as the leading part of any conversation before a relationship is established. We encourage you to do the challenging work of holding on to and communicating the following standard to others: You don't have to look, act, or believe like us to belong. This is essential to help make the sensitive connecting communication in the building trusting relationships process go smoother, and faster.

A Packing List for the Journey

Allow us one more metaphor. Both of us enjoy camping and spending time outside. The Bonner family enjoys using their RV, and the Sturtevants are lifelong tent campers and backpackers. We both have camped in an assortment of seasons and locations, requiring a wide variety of preparations. Some campgrounds offer plush facilities while others have uneven sites lacking facilities. Backcountry trips through the desert with little water or cold overnight treks up and into the mountains provide different challenges. No two trips are ever the same: quick overnights close to home; long multi-night treks; idling in an RV in snarled city traffic; sharing the trail with bears, raccoons, and other hikers; a variety of weather, often unpredictable and uncertain even on day one. And yet that particularity and unpredictability do not mean that we do not plan. In fact, when getting ready for most trips, we pull out a well-worn packing list, and it becomes our guide for preparing. The list is a helpful starting place from which we can adjust, particularize, and say a hundred times, "Oh yeah, I forgot one of those last time and sure wish I hadn't!" Once again we acknowledge that our shared experiences and learnings are not universal, nor are they universally transferable.

No two congregations are the same. And even the same congregation is not the same congregation at a different time in a different context with different participants and leaders. However, as we offer our findings, perhaps a packing list would be helpful. In the following pages, we offer a starting point for your journey (or maybe a refuel, if you are already halfway there!). We share some ideas about how you and your congregation might "pack your bags" wisely and expectantly. What provisions do we think you might need for your trek? What have you learned through your experiences when you have said, "Oh yeah, I wish I had done that last time!" As any experienced camper or backpacker knows, space and weight matter! You don't want to carry what you aren't actually going to need. So if some of these suggestions are less helpful than others, feel free to set them aside and leave them at home. What follows is a list of ideas and principles you might choose to gather to create an effective, peaceful, gracious decision-making process. We hope our list helps you prepare for your journey!

Intentional Leadership

Cultures of trust and collaboration do not just happen. Identify the natural leaders within the subgroups of your church and invite them to join the process as coleaders. Meanwhile, be sure to include voices from the margins, even if they have not been in prior leadership roles. Clergy can be involved directly as active members of this coleaders group or can remain on the sideline as a coach. Either way, pastors will have an active role in the process through their preaching. This role is important enough that we have taken an entire chapter to talk about ways the pulpit and preaching life might engender trust. Consider carefully, given denominational and congregational polity, what the expectations for the preacher beyond the pulpit might include. Continually remember, we are all on the same team, the same family, not opposing forces or enemies.

Continue collaborating in this coleaders group only until it has healthy functionality as members demonstrate an ability to abide by the Communication Covenant found in chapter 7. As well, recognize that some of these leadership and listening skills are not innate to all people. There is no shame in seeking out training opportunities for consensus-building, discernment, or communication skills. This may make for a longer process, but it also makes it more likely a healthy process with a positive outcome.

Spirituality and Spirit-Led Discernment

Every step must be taken with an open attitude of discernment. Use Scriptures, prayer, bi-directional open communication, connection, and interaction with the Holy Spirit to keep the process spiritually focused and connected to God. Our example of the composite church West Bay in chapter 6 models some good spiritual practices for Spirit-led discernment. Prayer is key to every step of the process. Another must for participants is to open their minds by letting go of preconceived judgments and conclusions. The wise do not start a discernment process at the conclusion. Instead, they invoke the words of the old hymn, "Open my eyes that I may see glimpses of truth Thou hast for me."[13]

Clear and Well-Communicated
Practices for Transparency

Life is a journey—not a competition. Inform participants, especially at the beginning, that the process will be gradual and at times may seem slow and uncomfortably contentious. That does not mean that the issue cannot be settled with conflicts of opinion resolved in a peaceable manner. Instruct participants that all work is to be done during the set, agreed-upon meetings. None of the work will be done in hallways or the parking lot or in private, including by email, telephone, conversations, or meetings. Assure everyone that no one will be using power-grabbing moves to orchestrate a quick or deceptive voting event to get the decision or outcome they want. Everything is to be done above board as everyone will be working together and doing their best to keep all participants informed about what they are doing. We recommend that each subgroup provide written reports on their activities and progress to the church clergy and lay leaders/ council, available for review by anyone. Plus, general reporting of progress should be made to the whole congregation through oral reports and newsletters.

Strengths-Centered Gratitude

What are the positive attributes of individuals and the whole group? The best foundation is one built on understanding strengths and assets at the table. Use positive reinforcement, including overt recognition of virtues and accomplishments, while considering carefully how to discuss shortcomings and challenges. You can use the abundance perspective to build a healthy, relaxed, productive culture. An environment focused on mutual respect and nurturing with positive reinforcement highlights individual and systemic strengths and potential. This is not a win-lose situation nor a zero-sum game. It is about being the hands, feet, ears, and mouth of Christ on earth (see Matthew 25).

A strengths- and assets-based approach is possible from the pulpit as well. How might you name "good news in the world" in your own congregation? When a congregational system is feeling at odds or uncomfortable, naming the church's strengths can be powerful. Think about the congregation's history, specific ministry successes, or week-to-week strengths that you have seen. Congregations that have a long-shared history (i.e., multiple generations) might need to be reminded that they have been here before. Churches do not survive over hundreds of years without figuring out how to deal with cultural divisiveness and controversy. Name that strength from the pulpit. Instead of being overwhelmed or afraid of what is ahead, build on what has already been accomplished.

Reappraisal Sharing

Engage in recognizing and building on past successes—reappraisal sharing. Discuss what was valued in the past, and honor it. Search the church archives or written history of the congregation for reminders. Get together and ask, "What were the strengths that enabled the accomplishments of this church in getting beyond difficult or divisive times in the past?" Record a list of these strengths, share them with everyone, and keep them posted as reminders throughout the process. Sharing recognition and gratitude for work well done goes a long way. At the center of cultural divisiveness is suspicion, criticism, and judgment of the other, so practice the opposite: look for what others are doing well through the process and commend them, positively reinforcing their strengths, while modeling healthy communication skills.

Equality and Alterity

Build your congregational process on the values of equality and equity, affirming the worth and accepting the value of all voices. Let everyone know they are welcomed into the process and that their values, priorities, and experiences will be accepted and considered. Remind them repeatedly that their voice is needed in this shared process and that it will be heard. Sharing and hearing are the purpose of this process. Do not be like the Jews in Antioch who not only did not agree with what Paul and Barnabas were teaching but also "stirred up persecution against Paul and Barnabas, and drove them out of their region" (Acts 13:50). An elastic church congregation seeks to grow relationships through the practice of respect, welcoming, hospitality, inclusion, and collaboration.

Boundaries—Clearly Set and Consistently Enforced

State the explicit expectation that participants will honor the commitment of mutual respect with each other. Then inform them that group leaders will politely intervene as necessary to assure that all communication and interactions continue to be healthy and constructive. We highly recommended that two persons from the leadership team be present for all open discussions and work to consistently enforce this expectation.

This boundary setting can become even more complicated in the age of social media. It is essential to have the boundary of keeping the process all in house. Remind congregation members not to air their opinions or grievances about other members, leadership, or church planning or process online. Crossing such boundaries increases anxiety and invites input from those who are not committed to the congregation's relationship network or wellbeing. While healthy public conversation around controversial issues has value, engaging with those who are not covenanted to communicate within set boundaries can quickly become counterproductive.

Awareness of Emotions

Churches will benefit from educating their congregations in emotional awareness and mature emotional health. Maturity and emotional intelligence are seen as truth—the inner, mature self, the whole person, including the soul. Regardless, honest disclosure of oneself is required to be a whole person. Emotional honesty can be attained by teaching awareness and constructive expression of emotions. Emotions tell us more about truth in the moment, the reality of self in relation to the social environment, than our rational minds' reasoning or logic does. We can rationalize anything. Leaders can start by teaching self-awareness of personal emotions being experienced (e.g., mad, sad, glad, insecure/ anxious, repulsed, guilty, proud) prior to them being expressed. Then teach strategies for managing emotions in positive, helpful ways that are in the best interest of all. Practice emotional intelligence with empathy, including sensitivity to the feelings experienced by others. This brings it into the social interaction realm. This reality check of communicating about intuitive feelings and emotions with others helps individuals discover the best version of themselves. Focus on emotional truth enables a systemic process of trusting each other to work together, and assertive action gets the job done in a healthy way of attaining justice for all concerned. Churches could benefit from having the security and confidence to start an all-church decision-making process, despite the risk of conflicting values, resistance, and opposition.

Mindfulness

Express expectations for mindfulness. Mindfulness is focusing one's awareness—noticing what is happening in the moment without judging. Just relax, rather than tensing up as if preparing for a fight. These processes go much better when everyone can stay mindful and calm to build trust by staying in the moment, here and now in the present context. Even when discussing the past and the future, you need to keep the focus on "What does that mean to this church body today?" No discussion should digress into focusing on others who are not present or not directly involved in the church's process. Each person must speak only for themselves and not reference persons not present.

Mindfulness can be taught from the pulpit, and teaching mindfulness prayer practices might also be helpful. One example is based on the call stories of Old Testament prophets: "Here I am." Encourage participants to offer themselves to God, saying, "Here I am in my body. Here I am in my thoughts. Here I am in my emotions." Through such prayer practice, the congregation will learn mindfulness in the Spirit.

Curiosity

Be curious rather than critical. Be open to new perspectives with empathy, listening, exploring, and learning more about fellow participants. The church can be an ideal place for learning about people and their purposes. We can be enriched by new experiences and learn to modify our expectations and demands in a collaborative manner.

Along those lines, continue to be learners when it comes to the tenets of an elasticized ecclesiology. Many people are writing about the church, trust, and alterity—don't just take our word for it. The bibliography at the end of this book can serve as a continued reading list. We invite you to be curious and follow that curiosity deeper into some of these authors' ideas. Be ready to learn about new concepts and differing ideologies. Intentionally read and research those with whom you are prone to disagree. Pay attention to what might trigger you and set boundaries appropriately. When you are able, allow yourself to be pushed beyond what is intellectually and emotionally soothing—get out of your comfort zone!

Empathy

Create a culture of help first. When you are dealing with a difficult issue or process, first think of alterity with empathy, "What does the other need?" Look around and notice how others are also struggling. Use empathy to communicate, connect supportively, and compassionately assist them. One can shift focus away from self-absorption by using the strengths perspective and asking, "What are you needing?" Once that is clarified, ask, "How would you like me/us to help you with meeting that need?" Another element of empathy is to consider others' perspectives and why they might show fear or concern about your opinion or perspective. Maybe something has happened or is still happening in their families that triggers fear or anxiety in emotional conversations. Perhaps something is happening that has nothing to do with the issue at hand but serves to distract or exhaust their ability to stay healthy and mindful. How might you practice empathy for all participants?

Finally, empathy can be a shared strength when it leads to the hands-on mission to which Christ calls us. We have seen congregations at each other's throats in business meetings set aside their differences and serve arm in arm at the local soup kitchen. Shared empathy for others outside of the congregational system is a powerful unifying force. Serving next to another builds trust.

In addition to shared conversation, perhaps a congregation might plan an intentionally shared congregational mission, even pairing the two experiences together. Practicing and debriefing shared empathy can be a powerful trust-building experience.

Constructive Criticism

Sometimes honest feedback includes suggestions for improvement. Offer positive suggestions only after trust is built and discernment practices convince you that your awareness and insights might benefit others without the risk of being hurtful or harmful. One helpful method is first to state two examples of what you like about them and what they are doing (positive reinforcement). Then, before offering a critique for improvement (constructive criticism), turn critical into constructive by asking if the other wants feedback and suggestions. If they say yes, share your thoughts regarding the things you believe will help them and be in the best interest of all involved. If they say no, then practice patience and kindness while saying, "Let me know if you change your mind or know of a better time for me to share my ideas." Then wait and focus on sustaining a peaceful attitude for a positive disposition while maintaining good working relationships throughout the process.

Remember that the pulpit is not the place for constructive criticism. Shame or guilt-inducing language is rarely effective, especially when offered in a context in which members have no voice to respond, which leaves hearers feeling helpless, untrusted, and distrusting. Prophetic preaching has its place, but the preacher should carefully consider content and form. Here is where stories might be a helpful homiletic medium.

Christ-Centered Connectedness

Obtaining consensus on agreeing to disagree and staying connected throughout the decision-making process is essential. Open, honest communication builds trust when people peacefully commit to remaining friends while working on sensitive, difficult, and potentially divisive issues. This Christ-centered commitment to stay connected transforms the conflict into decisive, constructive, productive action for the glory of God and the benefit of all. Once a decision is made by the congregation, everyone remains committed to mutually supporting one another while working together in following through to make the chosen action plan happen.

The preaching event is a critical moment for the practice of this connectedness. Through a shared homiletic, a congregation might find the unifying Spirit of God and biblical witness come alive in their midst. Shame-inducing language from the pulpit has the opposite effect, deepening divides and withering trust. The preacher has the potential to build trust and consensus through the homiletic of all believers, even when hard decisions must be made.

In the next chapter, we present case studies of various churches' pathways of trust. We discuss the patterns and processes we observed as the churches' socio-emotional relational systems responded to the new law of the land—legalized same-sex marriage. How have churches responded to LGBTQ+ persons and other diverse individuals living around them in their communities? Be curious about and open to exploring these churches' processes and see what you can learn from them.

NOTES

1. Douglas Avilesbernal with Linda Triemstra Cook, *Welcoming Community: Diversity That Works* (Valley Forge, PA: Judson, 2016), 62.

2. Standford University, The Martin Luther King, Jr. Research and Education Institute, "A Realistic Look at the Question of Progress in the Area of Race Relations," address delivered at St. Louis Freedom Rally, April 10, 1957, https://kinginstitute.stanford.edu/king-papers/documents/realistic-look-question-progress-area-race-relations-address-delivered-st.

3. Elizabeth Weiss Ozorak. "Cognitive Approaches to Religion," in Raymond Paloutzian and Crystal Park, *Handbook of the Psychology of Religion* (New York: Guilford, 2005), 223.

4. Michael Burch, Zoom interview with authors, March 23, 2022.

5. Grace Ji-Sun Kim, *Invisible: Theology and the Experience of Asian American Women* (Minneapolis: Fortress, 2021).

6. Jonathan Haidt, *The Righteous Mind: Why Good People Are Divided by Politics and Religion* (New York: Vintage Books, 2013), 52–61.

7. Haidt, 59.

8. Avilesbernal, *Welcoming Community*, 62.

9. Isabell Wilkerson, *Caste: The Origins of Our Discontents* (New York: Random House, 2020), 66, 386.

10. Michael Burch, Zoom interview with authors, March 22, 2022.

11. Kimberlé Crenshaw, "Mapping the Margins: Intersectionality, Identity Politics, and Violence against Women of Color," *Stanford Law Review* 43, no. 6 (1991): 1241–99, https://doi.org/10.2307/1229039.

12. Grace Ji-Sun Kim and Susan M. Shaw, *Intersectional Theology: An Introductory Guide* (Minneapolis: Fortress, 2018).

13. Clara H. Scott, "Open My Eyes, That I May See," *Celebrating Grace Hymnal* (Macon, GA: Celebrating Grace, 2010), #395.

6

Examples of Congregations' Processes: Three Pathways to Trust[1]

When the Supreme Court determined that same-sex marriage was legal (June 2015), it was thought to be settled once and for all for everyone—legally. However, the ruling invaded the consciousness of many members of Christian congregations across America, especially church leaders—lay and clergy alike. While some joyfully celebrated the new law, others were fraught with worrisome tension and anxiety. In some cases, people felt downright disgust and anger. Regardless of their beliefs, traditions, biblical interpretations, or policies, churches everywhere were forced to deal with that highly sensitive, emotional, and volatile issue—the fact that the new law had changed the status of LGBTQ+ persons at large. Although previous research had reported that LGBTQ+ people comprised 4 percent of the population, the most recent report showed that in the last decade that number has grown to 7 percent.[2] As openly LGBTQ+ people are a contemporary part of life, church leaders must respond. The question is: how can a congregation best respond?

Our studies examined different churches' responses to the factual existence of legalized same-sex marriage in the United States, which is a highly emotional, divisive issue—one with interpersonal trust at its core. The larger, more basic question remains: how should churches respond to others who are different? We focused on how lay and clergy church participants can best respond and interact with those who may not look, think, or act like them. Each composite church included provides an example of their response to alterity amid polarizing conflict. Although equality and inclusion are important, valued concepts and practices in a church, our intent is a neutral examination of how church leaders can optimally operate in managing and building trust in the presence of sensitive issues and divisive conflicts within their faith community.

To preserve anonymity while sharing our participant churches' processes, we present them through three composite examples. Each composite represents multiple similar churches. We have also protected our participants' anonymity by giving the churches and their personnel pseudonyms. Our three communities of faith are named Eastern Harbor Church (EHC), West Bay Church (WBC), and Journey Community Church (JCC). We use these churches as three important case examples for elasticized ecclesiology. Our hope is that you can see similarities to other congregations, including your own. These churches and their leaders are each walking their own path, each on their own journey of building trust, striving to be relevant, meaningful, and vital in their community.

These three mainline Protestant churches are all medium-sized, with memberships between one hundred and five hundred people. All are in urban/suburban locations. Each church has multiple pastors with the current lead pastors having been in their positions for several years. While two of them are predominately Euro-American congregations, Eastern Harbor Church has much diversity with a variety of racial, ethnic, and nation-of-origin differences among their participants and staff, making them a very mixed church, subverting the assumption that 11:00 Sunday is the most segregated hour of the week.

Viewing Congregations' Socio-emotional System

Our examination of multiple churches' lives through the lenses of holistic human interaction, alterity, systems theory, and orthopathy offers insights into how churches understand and deal with the reality that LGBTQ+ persons and other marginalized groups live among us. These observations and comparisons are intended to mesh with the churches' purposes of building trusting human relationships under the Holy Spirit's guidance to develop bonds for building the body of Christ. With these, a church can cocreate a healthy, vibrant community—peace within, peace between, and peace among, which is pleasing to our loving God. Thus, we can have peace with God.

Applying a systems perspective creates a shift in our awareness that restructures how we view human interactions—moving away from a superior position of fault-finding and condemnation to the position of equality with humility, hospitality, relationality, and power-sharing accountability. Viewing decision-making from the systems perspective changes a discussion's paradigm to one with more introspection and less projection of blame or scapegoating. In doing so, we see individuals as similar or alike and at the same time we can be aware of the power differential at the intersection of their behavioral interactions. We used this broader perspective to study patterns and processes of activities that were observed in churches as they responded to the new same-gender marriage law. For more depth on applying the Bowen Family Systems paradigm to communities of faith, see the work of Edwin Friedman, Peter Steinke, Michael Kerr, and Ronald Richardson.[3]

A congregation's socio-emotional system's processes are difficult to observe and understand, let alone describe. They often are invisible to observers and are mostly absent from the awareness of the persons experiencing them. This examination of multiple churches' lives through the lenses of emotional awareness, social intelligence, and systems theory offers a means for gaining useful insights. Below, we identify three distinct *Journey of Trust* models based on the churches and pastors we studied. We elaborate on these composite church models later in this chapter.

Synopsis of Three Churches' Journey of Trust

Here we briefly present a general summary of the three composite churches covered in-depth later. The three churches were in similar urban/suburban settings, although none is classified as an inner-city, downtown church. They were similarly medium-sized congregations, and like other mainline Protestant churches, each had declined membership from its previous high. All three had congregational-type polity within similar denominational structures. Although we studied additional churches, we excluded those most divergent from our composite examples. Churches of different sizes, settings, demographics, or polity may have some significant differences in outcomes. The challenge is for each church to seek and find its own path of trust-building to honor God, other, and self.

Pragmatic but Nonconfrontational Process

Eastern Harbor Church provides a model of a pragmatic but nonconfrontational process intended to preserve connectivity. The church demonstrates how a congregation's leaders can reach a decision without the emotional confrontation of an organized decision-making process. Advantages include the ability for current members to be pragmatically welcomed and included without forcing the issue onto congregation members who cannot personally commit to a church-wide policy or stay in a church that does. Disadvantages include a lack of clarity for LGBTQ+ persons about whether the church welcomes them or if only the handful of staff who have shown hospitality in these pragmatic ways do. This process runs the risk of feeling like "don't ask, don't tell." Some may perceive an unspoken "Don't talk, don't trust, don't feel" rule, which could impede full healthy functioning throughout the system. Alternatively, some in the LGBTQ+ community expressed that they do not want rainbow flags or being named/welcomed from the pulpit. The reason they gave was, "I want to be able to bring Grandma to my church."

Community and Consensus Process

A model of consensus in community process comes from West Bay Church. This model suggests, "We are going to be as expansive as we can be as long as we still stay together." It focuses on clarity of community more than policy clarity. The biggest advantage of the consensus model is that it emphasizes staying together and keeping the current membership but also presents a stance of "inclusion without affirmation." Their byline is that every voice will be heard, valued, and led to the point of consensus. They have kept more folks by agreeing to a less clear policy that allowed those initially opposed to staying. The main disadvantage is a less clear policy that may sound like, "We are a church that can perform same-sex weddings if anyone ever asks, and we will not punish pastors if they choose to do so." That may make it more difficult long-term to clearly explain to folks, "This is who we are." The lack of clarity runs the risk of speaking out of both sides of the mouth: "You (LGBTQ+ individuals) can come to the table but no dessert for you." Although the church may say, "All are welcome," the meaning is not fully clear.

Clarity in Policy Process

The Journey Community Church models a clarifying policy process. They demonstrate this with the clearest decision-making process, which revealed what their identity was: "We are a church that does same-sex marriages, as decided by our congregational decision (vote)." Advantages include the ability to say to new visitors and members, "This is who we are," and to say to LGBTQ+ persons and allies, "You can come to the table, eat, and have dessert!" The primary disadvantage, however, is that for those who cannot agree to that clear policy, it forces the issue of whether they will continue as members. Therefore, it risks the loss of members or even a church split. Churches following such a model could also risk operating from an assumption that "We are going to lose some members anyway, so we don't have to work so hard to listen to them or include them in the decision-making process." Also, some people may experience very hurt feelings, such as perceived breaches of trust and subsequent gut reactions among some during the decision-making process. That grievous loss of relationships can lead to a painful parting of the disaffected, with the pain experienced by those who stay as well as those who leave.

Let there be no mistake: we are not judging churches here. And certainly we are not elevating any one church above any other. Each church congregation is unique. Therefore, no one universal method or practice will work for all. The key is for the church body—laity as well as clergy—to actively work on finding their own identity, vision, and mission while working to attain and maintain trusting relationships among all participants.

Three Composite Churches and Their Decision-Making Processes

EASTERN HARBOR CHURCH—PRAGMATIC, ONGOING PROCESS

CATEGORY	SPECIFICS
Denomination/polity	Mainline Protestant/congregational
Location	Eastern US
Setting	Urban/suburban
Size	Medium (100–500 members)
Ethnicity	Mixed
LGBTQ+ signage	None
Leadership	Multiple pastors, lay leader, plus administrative council/board

Eastern Harbor Church sits in an eastern US urban/suburban area. It has a well-established and adaptive history. However, its membership has shrunk down to where it barely meets the criteria for a medium-sized church. Their worship style is a hybrid of traditional and contemporary. They do not appear to be an all-the-way welcoming and affirming church, as they do not have anything to indicate their receptivity to or affirmation of LGBTQ+ persons on any of their flagpoles, signage, or displayed literature.

When asked about LGBTQ+ persons and the new same-sex marriage law, Rev. Thomas Smith, senior pastor, said, "It has not been something we think we need to talk more about here (at this time)." He went on, "It hasn't been an issue here. We have had several LGBT [sic] persons here over the years and some had been in leadership positions: lay leader, treasurer, and even pastor." When questioned, Smith explained, "(That pastor) was not 'out' at that time, but everyone knew."

One distinctive aspect of EHC is immediately evident. Their mixture of races makes them an exceptionally diverse congregation as they are around 40 percent BIPOC. Their church includes African Americans plus persons with Latino/Latinx or AAPI (Asian) heritage, with a slight majority of white members. The pastoral team mirrors the church's diversity, as the senior pastor and other leaders within the church are also people of color. Reverend Smith shared, "For most of us, this is the most diverse social grouping we have ever been a part of in our lives." Their leadership includes associate pastor Rev. Martha Pasco and head lay leader Susan Johnson.

When we sought depth on their thinking about the issue of same-sex marriage and LGBTQ+ inclusion, Reverend Smith responded, "I am a little reluctant to have our church become fully *welcoming and affirming* because of our older members and some of our Black members as well. I'm not sure they are ready for it, and I don't want to limit evangelism. I want to attract people and help them broaden their minds. We have only a couple of very opinionated members. Mostly we try to get along to go along—so we can continue moving forward."

Reverend Smith explained EHC's decision-making process on same-sex weddings this way: "The question was brought up by a layperson on the council who asked, 'What are we going to do about LGBT weddings since they are now legal?' So I taught a course on what the Bible teaches about homosexuality. There are questions today that have no answer in the Bible. There is nothing in there about mutually loving LGBT relationships. It only addresses prostitutes and eunuchs." Reverend Smith indicated that about one-fourth of the congregation participated in the five class sessions. Early in the process, he reported no pushback, but he later stated, "There were two men, each of a different race, who voiced different opinions [in opposition to what I was teaching]."

Eastern Harbor Church's lay leader, Ms. Johnson, provided a different perspective: "We are a community of silence—no discussion. I went to the pastor's class, and it was okay. There was some discussion among the participants. I know there were at least a few who were against . . . LGBTs in the church, but they didn't say much." She elaborated, "We don't really talk about any other issues in the groups I'm in here—things like social justice issues." After contemplating for a moment, she concluded, "It was the same for the Bible study group I attended in the past." We interpreted that to mean that no one was willing to take risks—to rock the boat, so to speak—to talk about divergent opinions or interpretations, especially regarding controversial issues. Thus, her statements provided examples of systemic avoidance of controversial discussions within EHC by both clergy and laypersons. Are they a socio-emotional relational system resisting change, or are they quietly, gradually enacting it?

Significantly, Eastern Harbor is also the church that has a larger percentage of participants who are openly in the LGBTQ+ community—yet they are still a small minority. They even administered at least one wedding for same-sex persons. They reported that wedding plans had been discussed in the church's council meeting "without any problem—no objections were expressed." All interviewees reported that they had not heard any negative comments about the wedding among the congregants.

Reverend Pasco reported that one LGBTQ+ couple had some of their closest friends from church stand up with them at their wedding. They had openly invited people from the church with a general announcement and had especially encouraged certain ones to attend, as the couple thought they would be supportive and thus safe. About ten church members had attended that wedding. However, one African American woman whom they had especially invited did not attend. She had expressed that she was "not ready yet." That last statement was congruent with what Rev. Cliff Matthews Jr., a Black pastor in a different church, told us:

> *Homophobia has been preached in the Black church for so long, we have to gradually back into dealing with it [LGBTQ+ persons in the church], rather than forcing the conversation. In my church, some like it, some don't, and most don't give a damn. We are like the Hebrews traveling to the Promised Land. Some want to go back to Egypt. Some want to march forward to search for the Promised Land. Most are just doing what their prophet, Moses, told them to do. In the Black church, the minister is both preacher and prophet—the community depends on the pastor to tell them what is right—what to do.[4]*

This statement contextualized Reverend Smith's sensitivity and insight as he resisted pressing the question or having more discussions in his mixed-race church at that time.

Rev. Martha Pasco, the associate pastor, was positive and upbeat as she expressed that most people in their congregation were loving and caring. "We notice when someone is missing and check on them. But I want us to be more open and affirming, instead of just being 'loving.' The thing is that they [LGBTQ+ persons] want to hear it said that they are affirmed—just as they are. And not just hear an 'I love you' that does not affirm them specifically." With tension evident in her voice, she expressed concerns about the future of the church by saying that they must change the way they do things to continue—to be sustainable.

> *We are planning on starting new ministries that hopefully will improve our situation. But I'm also scared of our church opening*

*up and honestly talking about it and trying to make decisions
on this controversial issue, because we have not been talking
about it. We are "don't ask, don't tell." One LGBTQ+ couple we
married is bringing friends here, who we think are also in the gay
community. I would have loved it if we were open, so they would
have known from the beginning that they are welcomed and
affirmed—so they can feel safe here. I am concerned that someone
may say something that would hurt them. I know that healing
takes such a long time.*

Reverend Pasco summarized EHC's current position well with
her goal of continuing to build trust in their mixed congregation by inviting, making space for, welcoming, and affirming
all, especially those who were different—no exceptions. The
big question for EHC is the same as that for many churches in
North America today. Will their evangelism attempts be effective enough, their preaching vital and enlivening enough, and
their polity open enough for the church to build trust and grow
to be sustainable in the future—even just five or ten years down
the line?

Strengths: The East Harbor Church's socio-emotional system functioning was summarized well with the pastor's statement, "We go along to get along." Indeed, this church has many
positive qualities with successful outreach to diverse groups of
people that resulted in an exceptionally mixed congregation
among them. They were mixed in terms of race, gender in leadership, sexual orientation, and theological perspectives. The pastors and a significant portion of their congregation were of like
mind—more progressive and inclusive. The EHC clergy and lay
leader all expressed awareness that some, a minority, opposed
being openly welcoming and affirming. Yet, EHC pastoral leadership demonstrated their position by actions rather than words
alone by inviting, welcoming, and including LGBTQ+ persons
and openly performing marriages of a same-sex couple.

They also had acted out their values with a few sermons
specifically stating their church should be "welcoming and

affirming of all [meaning every human being]." Church personnel indicated that the LGBTQ+ persons in their congregation had not called for a more outspoken stance by the church or for a vote in the matter. In fact, some had said specifically that they did not want to be in a church where LGBTQs were singled out and spoken to from the pulpit on a regular basis.

Weaknesses: Eastern Harbor Church's primary weakness is the minimal amount of structured, facilitated ways their church participants can openly communicate and interact to build trust while directly dealing with controversial issues and values conflicts. They shared that at least two of their members had spoken up in disagreement with the lead pastor's teachings during their brief educational process. It appeared that the opportunity for more dialogue was constricted, given that the brief class ended and there were no subsequent learning or discussion meetings.

Although they have several LGBTQ+ persons participating in their church, the socio-emotional relational system of East Harbor is constricted. Has it been bound by an unwritten rule of no public talking, like "don't ask, don't tell"? Same-sex marriage was discussed briefly in their council meetings without a vote being taken. It is possible that budget considerations were a major part of why they were not taking risks by having open discussions on a controversial topic. Also, all personnel interviewed at EHC expressed awareness that they had other ongoing divisive conflicts that were unresolved in their church at that time. Perhaps their socio-emotional relational system was in a fragile state that could not accommodate direct discussions regarding any of their ongoing issues. Added to that was the long history of homophobia preached in the African American churches, which may have hindered some members' willingness to accept changes.

Eastern Harbor Church's constricted process was initiated by a church council member asking the reality-based question, "What are we going to do about legalized same-sex marriage?" What if the pastors, Smith and Pasco, responded by involving more church participants in an intentionally planned learning, discussion process, starting with the council? What about having open forums at different times and places that created space for the congregants to feel safe in sharing their opinions and feelings? Those forums could include a panel of LGBTQ+ Christians—possibly participants in their own church. EHC could have invited outside speakers, perhaps leaders from other churches who had experienced a decision-making process. Granted, every action involves risk. However, in those well-developed, open sharing and learning spaces where everyone was invited to express themselves constructively, they could require strict communication guidelines with consistent enforcement that would prevent negative personal attacks and escalation of conflict to make progress in building trust amid changes (see Guidelines for Healthy Trust-Building Discussions in chapter 7).

WEST BAY CHRISTIAN CHURCH—A UNIFIED PATH TOWARD CONSENSUS

CATEGORY	SPECIFICS
Denomination/polity	Mainline Protestant/congregational
Location	Western US
Setting	Urban/suburban
Size	Medium (100–500 members)
Ethnicity	Predominantly Euro-American (white)
LGBTQ+ signage	"All Are Welcome" (no rainbow flag)
Leadership	Multiple pastors, lay leader, plus administrative council/board

West Bay Christian Church is a medium-sized, urban/suburban church with a primarily Euro-American congregation located in the western part of the United States. Their decision-making process regarding the newly legalized same-sex marriage was begun by their lead pastor, Rev. Carol Culver, who brought the question to her staff and their lay leader, Mike Brand, soon after the Supreme Court decision. As they discussed the controversial issue, Reverend Culver expressed that she felt the need for guidance regarding the implications and impacts of the ruling on their congregation. They agreed to broaden the discussion to include the church council.

Reverend Culver and lay leader Brand brought those concerns and questions to the congregation's administrative council. The pastor called it "seed planting." For the next three months, the church leaders explored "what homosexuality and same-sex marriage meant to us and our church, using a structured process of healthy dialogue." At those council meetings, which were open to anyone, attendees shared diverse opinions and beliefs on the subject. There was disagreement on the direction the church should take.

In their early meetings, the staff and the council discussed the new law and the possibilities it presented. How would they respond to a request for a first same-sex marriage in their congregation? They did not have anyone in their church who was "out" as an LGBTQ+ person at that time, and it became evident to them that their church had not adequately explored the issues they called "homosexuality" or "sexual orientation." Thus, questions remained unanswered. Were they or could they become accepting, welcoming, including, and affirming of all persons, including those who identify with being in the LGBTQ+ community?

The WBCC council gathered in a special retreat for sharing and reflecting on what grounded their understanding of God and what was most important in their life of faith and community. Reverend Culver told them, "This has much to do with shaping who we are and who we want to be as a people of God as we move into the future." The council agreed that the church needed to decide as soon as possible and that the process should include the whole congregation.

Pastor Culver shared what she had discovered by "running into brick walls while trying to do my normal pastoral work." She asked questions of her congregants, and after her two-year process of exploration, concluded the systemic distrust was related to past conflicts in the congregation. She reflected:

People felt loss and were grieving because they didn't have the necessary skills to navigate the conflict—not even in their own family issues. So, they couldn't communicate to resolve conflicts in the church. I made sure that my view was not what was out front. I had studied social processes in building communities and the importance of "belonging" and learned to make sure that everyone feels like she has a voice. We said that all the time— write a letter, make a call—it can be anonymous, but everyone must have a voice.

Next was an all-church, open meeting, where they introduced the idea of a whole church conversation on sexual orientation and same-sex marriage. Small-group discussions were initiated around tables to explore and share personal feelings about starting that conversation. The pastor said that she had taken no stance on the issues. "That irritated a few people—but they are folks who like to blame everything they can on the pastor. Plus, I didn't feel like it was my position to tell them what to believe. We needed to walk through it together." Though not unanimous, the majority of the council and the membership concurred that the church should have more conversations regarding possibilities regarding same-sex marriages; and that it should be in "an open, structured, thoughtful, and safe environment throughout the process."

Within a few months, the WBCC council formed the "graceful engagement team," a term borrowed from *Building an Inclusive Church: A Welcoming Toolkit*.[5] Although the tool kit was used in the first steps of their process—the initial assessment and defining how they were to communicate and work together— they did not strictly follow the tool kit recommendations during the rest of their process.

Their team was composed of a balance of genders, ideologies, and theologies. They were intentional in having all sides represented, stating, "We wanted persons who could think holistically." Some members were from the congregation (i.e., were not on the staff or church council). The graceful engagement team was to collaborate with Reverend Culver in shepherding the congregation through a planned process for healthy dialogue and education on the issue of sexual orientation, same-sex marriage, and what it means to be a welcoming, open, and affirming congregation—or not. They were instructed to provide counsel and support to the pastoral staff and each other by displaying "a loving, caring, and open spirit."

From the beginning, Reverend Culver provided guidance on discernment practices and asked each member to commit to a prayerful process of reading the Scriptures, meditating, and praying daily to listen for God's guidance on the following questions: "God, what is your yearning for our church? What would you have us do? God, how should we move forward? How would you have us grow spiritually?" This process—reading, questioning, and prayer—was to help the church move forward in decision-making while being open to whatever the outcome would be.

The graceful engagement team met regularly, and they intentionally decided they would take enough time to explore the matters sufficiently. They viewed YouTube videos, including David Gushee speaking on "Changing Our Minds."[6] They read books, researched articles, and talked with other churches. They also considered the processes other churches had gone through as part of their decision-making. In their team meetings, they each shared what they had gained from their time spent in study, prayer, and reflection.

The engagement team reviewed what they had learned from other churches, including the outcomes. From there they discerned what process they believed was best for their congregation. With consensus, they planned an in-depth series of group learning opportunities for all church participants to attend. Reverend Culver and the graceful engagement team reiterated throughout their process, "Anyone at any time can contact one of us to express their views or ask questions—no matter what they are."

The congregants were reminded by the graceful engagement team at each all-church gathering that they, as a church, valued diversity in thought and mind. The team also emphasized that they come from a variety of backgrounds, generations, scriptural interpretations, and ways of understanding and living out their faith. They shared that the reason they were moving forward with this topic and dialogue was that, thus far, most persons involved agreed it was time to further explore the topic. To provide guidance for the church members in this process, the team developed their own tools for healthy dialogue (similar to Guidelines for Healthy Trust-Building Discussions in chapter 7).

Pastor Culver followed up on each communication she received and offered to hear the congregants out in private discussions. She commented that those who were very opposed to any kind of acceptance of same-sex relationships were the toughest interpersonal interactions and elaborated, "I've always said that if someone is unhappy, I want to know. Then, the really harsh stuff showed up in my office. Frankly, it was so harsh it was really tough for me, but I survived." Thus, this pastor showed compassion, vulnerability, and willingness to take risks.

The WBCC lead pastor said the whole process was supported by healthy discernment, community-building practices, and group facilitation methods throughout:

> *Each and every conversation and gathering around this topic started with Scripture and prayer with a reminder of our healthy conversation tools. Everything we did was pulled together in writing and made available to anyone who wanted a copy for review. I wrote newsletter articles sharing where we were, how things went, and so on, but never said what I thought we should do or decide. I also never preached about it directly, other than sermons on what we are commanded to do as followers of Christ. For some, that was challenging enough.*

At the next all-church meeting in WBCC, congregants gathered. The engagement team presented their discussion questions. Participants were told that everyone around the table had an opportunity to share their voice if they wanted. For those who did not like speaking in a group, notecards were on each table for them to respond in writing. The gist of all comments in each small group's conversations was written down by the scribe chosen by each group. They handed in the notes, and the lead pastor read them out loud to the whole group without naming the source. Then Reverend Culver moderated any questions and discussion around that statement until nothing more was to be said.

Next, the graceful engagement team planned and scheduled a series of "learning and discussion" sessions. Their first open learning and discussion sessions were led by a professor who taught principles for interpreting Scripture. Another professor then led them through a series of "listening conversations" regarding the Bible and human sexuality. Those conversations also included an LGBTQ+ Christian—a member of another church who shared their personal journey.

The following session featured a health professional presenting the physical and psychological aspects of "homosexuality and sexual orientation." This presenter shared what the medical and science field of study had learned about gender identity and same-sex orientation, including scientific evidence on whether being same-sex attracted (LGBTQ+) was a choice. Reverend Culver reported that those meetings all concluded with lively, open discussions facilitated by herself.

WBCC's next all-church learning and discussion opportunity was a town hall–style gathering. They heard from two pastors with differing views, on their own congregations' journeys in decision-making regarding the same-sex marriage question. They were asked how and why their churches landed where they did. One pastor said their congregation's careful, intentional process discerned their final decision "to be welcoming, open, and affirming of same-gender loving relationships and marriages." The other pastor told of their church's process of study, discussion, and discernment. In the end, they decided "to be welcoming of all persons but not open to or affirming of same-sex relationships or marriage."

On their overall process at that point, Reverend Culver related, "We did the best we could to provide information and opportunities for both sides of the discussion to be heard and considered. Throughout the year, we checked in with the church council regarding how the congregation was feeling regarding our decision-making process. We asked for anything they might want to share, whether something they heard or their own views and feelings."

Because they were committed to hearing all voices, the team developed a survey covering a variety of questions on "homosexuality, same-gender marriages, and how the church should move forward on these matters." They sent it out electronically by email and sent hard copies to all who did not have email as all were invited and highly encouraged to participate (see appendix B: Example Survey). They reported very good responses on the survey, which they believed represented a good cross-section of the congregation.

WBCC's graceful engagement team reviewed and discussed all the input they had gathered in the long, seemingly slow process. They then discerned the will of God for the congregation. After a review of their existing policy, they reported their conclusion. They found little basis to distinguish between heterosexual, homosexual, or sexually abstinent members in membership or leadership opportunities. They pointed out that all members were permitted to participate in congregational life on the same basis as any other church member regardless of sexual orientation or gender identity. Also, all participants have the opportunity for membership, baptism, leadership, ordination, and marriage based on individual merit and the discernment of those elected to governance positions. They explained that their policies explicitly stated that a pastor may discern whether the performance of any wedding is permissible. They also emphasized that a member's disagreement with the pastor's discernment was not a basis for the dissolution of the pastoral relationship. This was one of the most significant parts of their determination. It protected the pastors from those who may disagree with their decision to perform a same-sex marriage. Furthermore, the meeting concluded with the establishment of a covenantal responsibility that, regardless of whether they agreed or disagreed, all were bound to demonstrate Christian love to others.

The church council accepted this policy review statement in full at their next meeting. It was followed by an all-church meeting to present their decision. Reverend Culver described it this way: "Again, everyone was gathered in groups of seven to eight. As usual, they had just heard an upbeat sermon on what it means to be a community—living and loving the way Jesus taught us to live. What does it mean to be committed to caring about others—even those who are different?" The team gave the policy review statement to parishioners and asked for feedback. Culver explained, "It was amazing! Folks who were opposed in the beginning to even talking about the topic got up and shared how spiritually transforming the process had been for them. Others shared how they recognized their personal struggles with judging others and that they discerned they needed to work on their own problems first." The pastor reported that a Black congregant told the group that WBCC was the only place in the 1960s that would marry him and his wife because of their mixed color and ethnicity. He had originally been against same-sex marriage, arguing that it was not scriptural. Culver concluded, "Others shared that through our process they had realized that they needed to be more open and welcoming. Truly, it was the most worshipful, beautiful meeting I've ever witnessed!"

WBCC's pastor said that after everyone had expressed what they needed at that meeting, a vote was taken by a show of hands. More than a hundred people attended the meeting, and there were only a couple of opposing no votes. Staff reported that several members had said they would leave the church if it allowed same-sex marriages, but those members did not leave. Only two persons left their church after their vote on marriage equality, and they had not been among those who voted in opposition at the meeting. At least two more silently exited the church in protest before the vote, never to return.

The church's vote had shown agreement on the pastors' freedom to marry anyone without consent from the congregation. Thus, it protected the pastor's status, regardless of whom they chose to marry. Although their vote did not bar anyone from membership or serving in any capacity, did that mean they were a "welcoming and affirming" church?

Reverend Culver stated, "Ours was a different approach that focused on building mutual respect and trust. I knew that without strong leadership, the chances of success were diminished." Culver further clarified her perspective: "When I interviewed at this church, I shared my leadership style—unless expectations and limits are set, the group will attempt to dictate throughout the process, and things do not work. Sometimes as a lead person, you have to say no."

The WBCC process resulted in wide consensus approval of same-sex marriages in their church and by their pastors. And they had accommodated the opposition by stating their position as "welcoming and inclusive" rather than "welcoming and affirming" of any LGBTQ+ persons participating in their church. Their trust-building journey appeared to be an outcome of unity and consensus rather than division. Thus, they provided an example of conflict transformation—divided opinions coming to an agreement without aggression.

Strengths: West Bay Christian Church's socio-emotional, relational system functioned efficiently and effectively, meaning they reached their all-church decision in a two-year time span. They had effective leadership that formed a diverse team, which held together and partnered throughout to facilitate the experience despite all its emotional roller-coaster ups and downs. The graceful engagement team took one year to discern the best response for their church before inviting the whole congregation into the process and used a gradual, step process of getting an increasing number involved at each phase. Perhaps their process was more focused, continual, and productive during their journey of trust-building and that enabled them to reach a decision-making point in less time. The leadership's planned structured learning and discussion activities may have enabled any resisters/ opposition to stay engaged and not thwart the decision-making process, which ended in near unanimity.

Perhaps the most striking difference in WBCC's process from East Harbor Church's was that the lead pastor maintained primary leadership throughout. Reverend Culver initiated an individual spiritual practice for discernment that was to be used by all. She was skillful in developing and implementing what she called "community" within WBCC, despite the challenge of opposite sides of the issue expressing strongly held opinions. She maintained an open-door leadership style throughout. Thus, many complaints were given to her to handle personally, rather than in public discussions. Carol Culver asserted that she did not preach a certain position on the question, other than following Jesus. Another difference was that WBCC had representatives from two churches that had completed their own decision-making process give presentations regarding their different final outcomes. Those presentations seemed to be an excellent way to provide an opportunity for church members to consider the matter and make inquiries about someone outside their own church. That factor appeared to add valuable objective information to their discernment process before their final decision.

Weaknesses: WBCC's process also had weaknesses, including that they had only a few minority persons in their congregation and no self-identifying LGBTQ+ persons as regular participants. They also concluded with not all agreeing on "affirming" LGBTQ+ persons, which was reported as "We landed on being welcoming and inclusive as a few church members said they were not ready to affirm homosexuals or their relationships." That resistance to *affirming* all people called into question their covenant, "We are all bound to show Christian love to others." Their decision-making process had proceeded at an appropriate pace, but it was less clear how much of the direction of the process was dominant leadership by the pastor. Furthermore, was their voting in an open group with a show of hands an authentic vote, or was it manipulation to assure consensus?

Public voting will always bear tremendous social pressure for conformity. Was their method of voting functionally silencing voices and suppressing the true position/opinion of those who were in opposition?

JOURNEY COMMUNITY CHURCH—A POLICY-CLARIFICATION DECISION-MAKING PROCESS

CATEGORY	SPECIFICS
Denomination/polity	Mainline Protestant/congregational
Location	Midwestern US
Setting	Urban/suburban
Size	Medium (100–500 members)
Ethnicity	Predominantly Euro-American (white) with some BIPOC
LGBTQ+ signage	None
Leadership	Multiple pastors, lay leader, plus administrative council/board

The Journey Community Church is also a midsized church in an urban/suburban setting whose membership numbers, like most others, are declining. This Midwestern city has a majority Euro-American (white) population with fewer than 20 percent being BIPOC. Journey Church's membership was whiter than their city. However, they did have two BIPOCs among those in leadership. Like the other churches, JCC is an established and adapting church that maintained its vibrancy by having well-attended, ongoing Sunday morning spiritual formation for all ages. These characteristics, along with its worship style, made JCC look like a traditional church despite its newer building.

The Journey Community Church's lead pastor, the Reverend Samuel Rickert, collaborated with the elected lay leader, Robert Marshall. The pastors, the lay leaders (a new one served the last year), and the laypersons on their guidance team (task force) were most active throughout this church's discernment and decision-making process. JCC was intentional about keeping up with cultural shifts as they had implemented a new strategic plan in previous years that had altered their structure. They described their adaptation to the contemporary, postmodern culture by having fewer elected positions and eliminating mandatory/regular committee meetings, which they now call "ministry teams." These teams seemed to be what pastor and church growth expert George Cladis was referring to when he wrote, "Ministry teams that are relational and network forming rather than bureaucratic have wonderful opportunities to grow and thrive in the postmodern world."[7] These two ingredients appeared to be vital for building trust in an active, welcoming church body. Would the outcome of JCC's decision-making process be traditional, progressive, or more of a purple mixture?

Soon after the 2015 Supreme Court decision on same-sex marriage, Reverend Rickert discussed the matter with the lay leader and informed him that he would not make their church's decision alone. They planned a special open evening meeting for church participants with the intent of getting the discussion started. More than fifty adults participated in the open meeting. They sat around tables for small-group discussions in their large fellowship hall. Reverend Rickert led the meeting by explaining the court's decision and stating that they were looking for direction from the church participants to assist in the decision-making process. The task for that evening was to discuss what legalized same-sex marriage meant to each of them as individuals as well as the significance for JCC going forward.

One table held an interesting mix of opinions on the matter. A woman came with Bible in hand and all the verses that mention homosexuality flagged.[8] She started the small-group discussion by proclaiming, "Homosexuality is an abomination that must be excluded from the church!" An elderly man started his sharing time with the statement, "I am a sinner. I'm not here to judge anyone. I had a family member who was gay, and we loved him just the same as everyone else in the family. Unfortunately, he got AIDS and passed away." Also at that table was a single woman who very somberly talked of having spent a lot of time and energy researching what the Judeo-Christian Scriptures said about same-sex attraction. She very gently and clearly explained her conclusion that attraction to the same sex was not forbidden by the Scriptures. "Rather," she said, "the Scriptures addressed specific behaviors that were unacceptable. Those behaviors were basically sexual abuse rather than a consensual, loving relationship." No others at the table seemed swayed by any of these expressed opinions. Most participants expressed tolerance and acceptance of same-sex marriage and stated that their life experiences had convinced them it was not uncommon.

In the end, all gathered, and each small group shared some of their discussions. One person stood before the group, stating that the Supreme Court majority's decision was very poor jurisprudence and expressed serious disagreement with the decision. A retired pastor responded, "I have studied the issue and am convinced that the Bible's Scriptures were not addressing any mutual-loving relationships. Instead, they focused on situations of exploitation that existed in ancient times." The meeting concluded with a general understanding and consensus that more work needed to be done before JCC would decide on whether to allow same-sex weddings in the church. However, they did not make any further plans that night.

The turnout for that first open meeting was impressive, as it was a strong showing for a controversial topic discussion meeting on a Sunday evening. That meeting revealed the existence of conflict among church members. Some were adamantly opposed to same-sex weddings in the church, while some spoke supportively. One participant commented afterward that, at his table, they had all been happy about the change in the law and wondered why it had taken so long. Only a couple of individuals expressed upset feelings over the matter as the majority had not been emotionally reactive to the topic during the discussion. Would that continue to be the case in this church's socio-emotional, relational system?

A few months after JCC's first open meeting, the discussion was reinitiated during a Tuesday night Bible study. One layperson led them through their own multiweek learning discussion and class-wide decision-making process. The conclusion of that process was a written request to the church's administrative council for the continuation of that learning, discussion, and decision-making work with the inclusion of the whole church body.

This church's leadership (the council and the clergy) considered and discussed the Bible study group's proposal and then agreed to their request. The council initiated a plan to involve the whole church in a learning, discussion, and decision-making process to be created and led by a specially formed committee. The council invited the entire congregation to their upcoming meeting to introduce this plan and to create a committee.

At the next all-church meeting, the conflict escalated as some laity loudly expressed their opposition to continuing any discussion/decision-making process regarding same-sex marriage. One person exclaimed, "It is very clear that the Bible says it is a sin! Why are we even talking about this?" Another sternly proclaimed, "We will not have a gay wedding in this church!" Others stated they thought allowing same-sex marriages was a good idea. Lay leader Marshall explained, "The council plans for a committee to be a task force studying both sides of the issue and reporting the results back to us." The study group was led solely by the lay leader in accordance with the council's decision that it would not include the clergy. Thus, a committee of lay volunteers was formed, some of whom were recruited to try to balance it with equitable representation of diverse ideologies.

All was moving along in JCC's socio-emotional system at that point as the committee began its work of discerning a position to recommend to the church. Given that they were not the ones making the final decision, they chose to call themselves the "guidance team." The team started strong with good participation among the ten members, reading and discussing various books and videos over the first six months. Over time, however, the group waned in participation and membership. Some stopped coming, and others moved away. Then the committee went through a discontinuous process of working on–not working on the matter, with only three meetings during the next year.

Another group of JCC members was working behind the scenes. They actively resisted the idea of having same-sex marriages in their church. They mostly focused on maintaining traditions. One woman was more outspoken in her opposition, along with other complaints. She expressed to multiple church members that she was very concerned because the preacher "does not preach the Bible." The woman even acted out her disagreement by exiting the sanctuary during the sermon delivery on at least two occasions. One time she had sat near the front of the church and demonstratively stomped out. Although most people in the church were not impressed or moved by that action, it had served to increase emotional tension in the church. The resister stirred the pot and increased the volatility of discussions among participants, which made the socio-emotional system more fragile and potentially explosive.

Some movement in JCC's process eventually came after significant changes occurred, including the installation of a new lay leader, Ruth Murphy, and the inclusion of the lead pastor in the guidance team's process. The discerned outcome of the guidance committee's process was an open-to-all learning and discussion series over three months. They requested a whole congregational vote on what had been discerned as the church's options regarding a response to the same-sex wedding questions. The church council readily adopted this plan.

During JCC's learning and discussion sessions, members who opposed same-sex weddings in their church remained mostly silent. They were even largely absent from all but the first and last of those meetings. However, they continued to communicate among themselves, primarily by email as well as in their small groups, throughout the process. At the last meeting, when the congregation voted on the options, they were not only present, but a few of them also strongly voiced their contentious disagreement.

Their incited turmoil escalated the tension in the church's final meeting to decide the matter as several outspoken critics expressed vehement accusations, such as, "The leadership never invited the conservative voice to be expressed in any of those discussions! Why did you force this vote now? You didn't have to do this!" Furthermore, they voiced complaints that the whole decision-making process, as well as the voting procedure, had been biased from the beginning. They alleged that a predetermined conclusion was planned not only to support "gay weddings," but also to join a national LGBTQ+ advocacy group. Moreover, they charged the church leadership with negligence for allegedly ignoring the question, "Is homosexuality a sin?" Those conflicts, finally being expressed outright, created intense conflictual tension with a mixture of emotions felt in the hearts of all who were present.

That day, as the process concluded, JCC's general membership's voting results were roughly 3 to 1 in favor of allowing same-sex weddings in the church and by their pastors. The top-ranked option was to endorse same-sex marriages and continue working as a church body on being *intentionally inclusive*. Their vote results appeared to reveal that the church had a more progressive identity—more bluish-purple than purple (perhaps violet or indigo). JCC had been through a long process, with the clergy and the congregation involved mostly in the beginning and end phases. The process was largely laity led. They acted as a church system that preferred to do their own difficult work of discernment and processing rather than it being done for them by the clergy. Some may see this as a major strength.

Throughout JCC's slow and gradual, largely lay-led process of decision-making, messages from the pulpit were aimed at developing trust in God, trust in each other, and trust in the outsider, the marginalized, and those who were different—without singling out LGBTQ+ persons or any minority. Those sermons encouraging openness to new possibilities, empathy, compassion, reconciliation, and graciousness in judgments regarding social interactions were founded on the Scriptures in the Holy Bible from both the New and Old Testaments. The preacher's charge to the congregation was to live and act in accordance with Jesus' teachings. At no point in their process did Reverend

Rickert disclose his personal stance on the marriage equality issue. That preaching was generally thought to have been very similar to the preaching at the WBCC but not as specific in addressing LGBTQ+ support as some sermons at EHC had been.

After a three-year decision-making process, JCC survived, but their participants had decreased in number due to the exodus of the 10 percent who were emotionally upset by the granting of marriage equality. JCC has not had an influx of LGBTQ+ participants, as they and other minorities remain a small percentage. Other than adapting to changes brought on primarily by the COVID-19 pandemic, they continued functioning much as they had before the vote, only with fewer people.

Strengths: JCC had an interesting mixture of shared leadership. Their work on the same-sex marriage law change was initiated by the lead pastor asking the congregation to join him in making the decision. After a study group petitioned them to do it, the JCC council decided it was best to form a committee to work on studying "both sides" of the issue. We see this language as reinforcing bifurcation in the congregation as it sets a single dividing line. The binary viewpoint sets up a battle between them. Instead, we urge people to view opinions on a continuum with various viewpoints. Then the task is not to win a debate or battle, but to learn, discern, and hopefully expand the church in numbers and broader services or mission work.

The JCC committee was to make a future recommendation for church action/inaction. And perhaps most significantly, they decided that the committee would consist only of the laity—no clergy involvement. Would that enhance the effective functioning of the committee, or did it interfere with it? Journey Church's *guidance committee* proceeded over the next two years with sporadic work in which some disagreements and frustrations prevailed. Was the lay leadership approach wise and efficacious? Other church leaders who specialized in this area told us that every congregation is different—what is right for one is wrong for another. There is no one-size-fits-all. Thus, it remains an open question.

Two years into their process, JCC's leadership changed the guidance team by including a new lay leader and inviting the lead pastor to join them. Soon after, they made a plan to move forward on this controversy. Roughly six months later, JCC returned to including the whole congregation in the discernment process. The ending of that process was a vote where all members could express their preference on the secret ballot.

On the plus side, their process was a theologically clarifying revelation of that church's identity—an intentionally more open-minded, progressive, welcoming, and inclusive community of believers. They were willing to break the long-held tradition of supporting only opposite-sex marriages in their congregation. Also, JCC's outcome was far from the worst of outcomes. Similar votes in other churches have resulted in a 50-50 split with an immediate, large-scale exodus. Such a vote is probably the worst outcome possible in terms of numbers and sustainability. One minister summarized it as "every pastor's nightmare."

Weaknesses: JCC's process was hampered because their task force—the study committee—faltered. The committee's active membership was depleted to a handful. And they had many months of inactivity when nothing was accomplished. In this case, the process may have suffered from a lack of clergy involvement, but we cannot say that would always be the case. Along with the alleged avoidance of the "Is homosexuality a sin?" question, the complaint of not inviting the conservative side was another possible weakness, as actively involving the entire congregation is essential.

Also, although their all-church discernment meetings were planned to include ample small-group and whole-group discussion time, it didn't always work out. The result was that half of the meetings included no small-group time and very little discussion time, which made them function as didactic teaching encounters rather than open learning/discussion and group processing.

Furthermore, JCC's decision-making process ended with a result that was not acceptable to all members. Dissenters or resisters continued to complain after the church's vote, and it was not long before at least 10 percent of the regular church participants left the church. Most switched their membership to a more conservative congregation where their values could prevail. That exodus was grievous not only to those who left but also to those who remained, especially the pastors. Given that no new church participants were gained because of that vote, their process netted a decrease in membership.

Comparing the Three Pathways Regarding Pastoral Authority

Our three composite churches provided different examples of pastoral authority and power-sharing—how the pastor participates in planning and enacting worship, administration, policy setting, and day-to-day practice decisions. This refers to far more than just preaching, as it focuses on leadership approaches and actions. It is more about the dynamics of human interactions—how the minister collaborates, especially the minister's relationship with the laity participants and attitude toward outsiders. To what degree does a pastor demonstrate a willingness for power-sharing and connecting with the people? Here we primarily examine pastoral participation in the decision-making process on this issue.

First we look at Eastern Harbor Church. Lead pastor, Reverend Smith responded to a layperson's question about how to work with the new law in their church by providing a brief, didactic process in which he taught his conclusions with a stance of authority. Then EHC's decision-making process, other than what was preached from the pulpit, nearly stopped. In that regard, the associate, Reverend Pasco, had preached a sermon where she was calling directly for all to be not only open and inclusive but also welcoming and affirming of LGBTQ+ persons. Soon after, the senior minister gave this directive to his associate: "We do not need any more sermons like that because no one is pushing back on that issue." He expressed praise for the sermon but also voiced his concern that he did not want sermons to upset anyone and risk losing members. The wisdom of that stance is open for interpretation, of course. Is that a control mechanism for the purpose of avoiding conflictual interactions and the inherent emotional turmoil that comes with them? Or is it sharing insight and wisdom regarding where the congregants are in their gradual process of change and granting them more time to accept new ideas? Perhaps EHC showed their embracement of alterity and inclusion more with their actions—their intentional welcoming of minorities, including LGBTQ+ persons, into their church services and performing same-sex weddings— rather than with their beliefs, sermons, or policies. Or it could be a complex mixture of all these factors.

The second case is from West Bay Christian Church. Lead minister, Reverend Culver maintained the primary leadership position throughout their process with very active direction, which was reported to have been collaborative in focus and purpose. She showed insight and sensitivity when stating, "In our experience and what I have learned along the way is the *sex* part is the big hang-up for many." Insight and wisdom such as this may have helped to facilitate WBCC's decision-making process, which was focused on consensus and unifying the congregation. However, could a lead pastor's presence and direction of every meeting be somewhat of an overreach that may intimidate some who possess differing beliefs or preferences? Could that stifle the open expression of divergent viewpoints? If so, pastoral presence, demonstrating authority nonverbally, would function to silence the opposition without words or direct actions, even though that may have been the opposite of the pastor's intentions. We can only raise the question, as it is difficult to know the meaning or cause of participants' passive resistance such as silence.

Our final case for this power-sharing comparison is from Journey Community Church. Lead minister, Samuel Rickert initiated JCC's process by establishing that the clergy would depend on the laity's guidance for how to respond to legalized same-sex marriages. He allowed the laity to work through the process as they chose, without his direction. That laity-led process involving many went on sporadically for two years without a decision-making plan. Thus, that process appeared to be unfocused with the purpose maybe not being clearly defined. In the last stage of their decision-making, laity leadership changed and Reverend Rickert was invited to become more directly active in the process. A few months later, JCC had their plan for an all-church decision-making process that included all-church group learning, discussing, and voting. Rickert of course was able to preach during the whole process, although he never stated a position on the question. Thus, JCC's pastor was part of a shared leadership process, which was gradual, long, and unfocused at times. Yet it eventually resulted in a conclusive decision-making procedure, which defined the congregation's policy on the question. One member commented after their process was concluded, "Our pastor allowed the processing by the whole congregation to work. That was his leadership style." Another said, "That was very different from the church I came from where the elders made all of the decisions."

OUTCOMES: WHAT HAPPENED DOWN THE ROAD?

With current statistics showing 7 percent of the US population now openly identifies as LGBTQ+, it is easy to project that the LGBTQ+ population will continue to be an important topic for churches and communities. By 2030 self-identifying LGBTQ+ persons could be 10 percent of our population or more—and this is a reality faith communities must connect with. The challenge is for each congregation to seek and find its own path of trust-building to honor God, other, and self.

Eastern Harbor Church: EHC's associate pastor explained their position well when she stated, "I pray and believe God is at work in our church. We are a gay-friendly church, but I can't say we are welcoming and affirming now." They have been walking the tightrope as they have stayed afloat and kept their doors open. They reported their participation numbers had not changed significantly as they continue to be a diverse, mixed congregation. Although they have been more diverse and more LGBTQ+ friendly and inclusive, they still have their struggles.

West Bay Church: The WBC consensus decision of being "welcoming and inclusive" has not led to any increase in LGBTQ+ membership or participation as it remains less than 1 percent. Their BIPOC participants are less than 3 percent of their congregation—roughly the same as before the vote. They have not displayed any signage that would indicate LGBTQ+ sympathies. They have not joined any national or local LGBTQ+ advocacy group, religious or secular. Three years after their vote, they have yet to have their first same-gender wedding.

In retrospect, we wonder if WBCC's welcoming and inclusive position was simply the right thing to do in their view as they were trying to keep their congregants happy. From an outsider or especially from an LGBTQ+ perspective, it appears that the feelings of those already in the church were more important than the feelings of those outside the church or even of newcomers who were different. Although it was acceptable to the membership, their decision did not appear to be something that functioned like a mission statement, which could lead to intentional changes in their behaviors in response to alterity. If so, that suggests that they still may not have connected to or served the people living in the margins of their locale.

Journey Community Church: JCC still has not regained the number of members who left, as none of them returned to their church and they have not experienced an influx of persons to replace them. However, a small number of the newly joined people at JCC said the church's LGBTQ+ policy was at least a part of the reason they joined. Also, some of those who were opposed to allowing same-sex weddings remained in the church but have not acted in an oppositional manner since the vote. Two and a half years passed before JCC performed their first same-sex wedding. They do not have any flag or signage displayed to indicate they are a welcoming and affirming church, but that message can be found on their website. They still have not joined an

LGBTQ+ advocacy organization of any kind—church-aligned or secular. In fact, none of the churches we studied had joined any such organization. Perhaps joining an advocacy organization is an even riskier, more sensitive, and potentially divisive issue than either holding a general welcoming position toward LGBTQ+ persons or performing same-sex marriages.

NOTES

1. Timothy J. Bonner, "Comparison of Four Midwest Congregations in Transition of Decision-Making on Same-Gender Marriage Using Bowen Family Systems Theory" (DMin diss., Central Seminary, 2018).

2. Jeffrey M. Jones, "LGBT Identification in U.S. Ticks Up to 7.1%," Gallup, February 17, 2022, https//news.gallup.com/poll/389792lgbt-identification-ticks-up. aspx.

3. Michael E. Kerr, *Bowen Theory's Secrets: Revealing the Hidden Life of Families*, Kindle ed. (New York: Norton, 2019); Edwin H. Friedman, *A Failure of Nerve: Leadership in the Age of the Quick Fix*, rev. 10th anniversary ed. (New York: Church, 2017); Peter L. Steinke, *Uproar: Calm Leadership in Anxious Times*, Kindle ed. (Lanham, MD: Rowman & Littlefield, 2019); Ronald W. Richardson, *The Church in Transition: Three Talks on Bowen Family Systems Theory and Dealing with Change in the Church*, Kindle ed. (CreateSpace, 2017).

4. Cliff Matthews Jr., Zoom interview with authors, March 20, 2022.

5. Rebecca Voelkel et al., eds. *Building an Inclusive Church: A Welcoming Toolkit 2.0* (Washington, DC: National Gay/Lesbian Task Force Institute for Welcoming Resources, 2013).

6. David Gushee, "Changing Our Minds: Top 10 Reasons Why I Changed My Mind on LGBTQ," YouTube, April 17, 2015, https://www.youtube.com/watch?v=7oO81hxbmGM. The book by this title is in the 3rd edition (2019) and includes a response to critics and a study guidebook for church leaders.

7. George Cladis, *Leading the Team-Based Church: How Pastors and Church Staffs Can Grow Together into a Powerful Fellowship of Leaders* (San Francisco: Jossey-Bass, 1999).

8. Those seven Bible verses have been called the "clobber passages" by these authors: Mel White, *Clobber the Passages: Seven Deadly Verses* (Palm Desert, CA: Wideness, 2020); and Colby Martin, *Unclobber: Rethinking Our Misuse of the Bible on Homosexuality* (Louisville, KY: Westminster John Knox, 2016).

7

Stopping to Ask Directions
When You Feel Lost

Some Step-by-Step Communication Guidelines

All human interactions require communication. Human beings conversing, interacting, and forming relationships can develop bonds—meaningful, caring, lasting connections through shared experiences. And those experiences will not all be positive, joyful, or conflict-free, even in a church. That is a fact of life. We all prefer, want, and at times may desperately desire our shared experiences to be pleasant, nonthreatening, and peaceful, which makes for enduring, mutually beneficial, trusting relationships. And trust must be earned through time spent in communication and meaningful interactions together. Trust is earned with integrity—when words are matched with observed, experienced actions.

Internal Safety for Everyone

Perhaps the most serious issue was brought up after the vote in one church when a participant said, "I didn't feel safe [enough] to express my opinion on the matter." The perceived safety of everyone is always a concern in group learning, discussion, and discernment processes. It hinges on the social and political balance of power, which requires emotional awareness, empathy, and agility in including and responding kindly to each other.

Every group is unique, and every group will have leaders—the outspoken ones. Also, every group will have those who are more reluctant to speak—the quieter ones. Although this may be a function of extroverted and introverted personalities, focusing on personality misses the point of always needing a balanced power differential for democratic processes to prevail justly and for all voices to be heard. These delicately sensitive challenges to leaders' capabilities require them to possess astute social and communication skills that must be learned.

Many Christians want to wear a happy face during their church participation; however, all humans possess a full range of human emotions. In addition to happiness/joy, there is fear/anxiety/insecurity, sadness/grief, anger/irritation/annoyance, and repulsion/disgust, as well as peaceful and secure, trusting feelings. Trust is a positive feeling that empowers self and others in the relationship to the benefit of the whole relational system. All human emotions exist on a continuum. And they can all be suppressed or repressed by any individual. Suppression is an avoidance response that blocks the feeling of emotion from a person's own awareness. Humans can also repress emotions, which is to intentionally or unintentionally hide their emotions from others by not expressing them directly. The nonexpression of true emotions is a dishonest avoidance technique. Either way, the emotion does not disappear. It just is not dealt with or expressed directly.

The ideal for emotional awareness, understanding, and expression is to use the two parts of our minds, the whole mind, simultaneously—rational, logical mind (the rider) and emotional, intuitive mind (the elephant). By using our whole mind, we can be fully aware of the emotional truth of our relationship in that moment and respect each other to work together for the common good. Honest interaction builds trust and creates opportunities for new possibilities where great things can be accomplished and huge obstacles can be removed. Thus, peace can be accomplished or maintained among the participants. Recommended guidelines for optimal communication are found below. Leaders are advised that they will do themselves and others a favor if they spend time reassessing their own communication skills before embarking on a journey in dealing with a controversial issue.

Healthy Socio-emotional Communication Skills

Church leaders, lay and clergy alike, need well-developed communication facilitation and group processing skills before starting an intentional group process dealing with sensitive issues, including an understanding of alterity and willingness to reach out to those in the margins. A good self-assessment for leader emotional aptitude and skill readiness is using the Communication Covenant (see sidebar below) as a prescreening tool. These guidelines are specific and may be more elaborate than what you want every participant to commit to. However, if any leader is uncomfortable or unable to covenant and utilize these communication guidelines, they should seek to develop and master those skills before proceeding. Coleaders should do the same.

Effective Practices for Transformative Trust-Building Processes

The church is home to its members, and a healthy home is a safe, familiar place. Any changes can shake that comfort in disturbing ways, which makes church work highly sensitive. We all need time to work at making changes in our perspectives, values, or behaviors. One caution is that some congregants will need more time and information before they can change their current mindset regarding a controversial issue. Although limits to the length of a change process exist, there is no need to rush the matter and make people so uncomfortable that they must fight back ferociously or flee out the door.

Churches do not practice trust-building by accident. Congregations that create inviting, welcoming, and power-sharing communities do so because they intend to integrate diversity as

Communication Covenant

When we seek truth, justice, mercy, and peace, we honor God, other, and self as we:

1. *Work together, not against each other,* with the goal being transforming conflicts into satisfactory, win-win outcomes for everyone. Thus, with this agreement, we avoid win-lose battles, and we can begin the way we want to end—united, healthy, safe, and strong.

2. *Embrace each one's uniqueness and individuality with tolerance of diversity,* as we remember our likeness, commonality, and traditions. We will show an understanding of hybridity—each has multiple parts that make their whole identity. Due to various life experiences, we may share some but not all traits.

3. *Work at collaborating to address each one's needs and solve problems.* We each accept responsibility for ourselves and for communicating our needs. We are accountable to the church family for our behaviors, but we can also advocate for our own self-interests. If we are struggling or have unmet needs, we will express it directly, with words.

4. *Act to communicate genuine respect, caring, and cooperation.* We will listen to each other with empathy and will not attack or seek revenge as we look for solutions instead of blame. If we see or hear another church family member struggling, we will offer to help, as needed, offering love with limits to empower the other but not to indulge or enable dependence.

5. *Communicate directly with honesty, assertiveness, and congruence* between our words, actions, and true feelings inside. Thus, we will not silently store or hide upset, disappointed, or resentful feelings, as that increases the risk that they would come out later in unintended, harmful ways. Also, we will be transparent and not talk negatively about others "behind their back" when they are not present.

6. *Only speak for ourselves using this I-statement formula: "I feel* (emotions: glad, sad, mad, hurt, scared, guilty, worried, disgusted,

etc.). I think (reasons for those feelings). I need (actions desired)." Next, we will ask, "How about you?" Then listen with empathy and compassion to understand, rather than form a reply or argument.

7. *Listen to understand alterity*—the other's situation, life experiences, cultural perspective, thoughts, emotional state, and needs. That is, putting ourselves in their shoes, so to speak. As needed, we will ask others, "Please help me understand your (view, position, experience) regarding this issue."

8. *Dialogue about this matter until we reach an agreement by consensus* (conflict transformation). If we are unable to attain that shortly, we will part with an agreement to disagree on that issue for the present time—hoping, planning, and praying to continue working until we reach a mutual agreement.

9. *Personally ask for a conflict transformation meeting* if conflicts have not been worked out. Then all involved come together with a mediator (selected by consensus) to work mutually for peaceful and harmonious, all-win conflict resolution to address intersectionality and the sharing of authority and power. Thus, we maintain hope for peaceful and harmonious conflict transformation without distress.

10. *Apologize* whenever this agreement is broken, directly to all who were offended as soon as possible.

11. *Work on making amends,* using the above skills with graceful humility, tolerance, forgiveness, acceptance, and support as we live out our religious or humanitarian values. Then we will move on, having learned life's lesson of the moment.

12. *Continue striving to work together* on becoming holistically healthy, constructive, and enjoying-the-moment individuals living with the least amount of stress (without animosity or fear) and giving thanks and glory to our gracious God.

they act out their inclusive values. Even though churches rarely overtly shun or turn away individuals, many faith communities have much to do to increase their intentionality toward alterity to avoid becoming exclusionary tribes. Daniel and Sharon Buttry teach conflict transformation using a river metaphor. They steadfastly remind us, "Change always comes from the margins, not the mainstream."[1] If we want change, we need to be aware of how intentional we are to connect with those in the margins, inviting them to join us, as well as how open we are to including them in all our activities. A good place for each church to start is with self-examination to determine, "How open and willing are we to improve outreach to alterity by connecting with those in the margins?"

A major issue facing adaptive churches is that some may express outright that they will not participate in any learning and discernment sessions regarding something new because they already have made up their minds about the issues. In their view, no amount of study or meetings will change their minds. A position of disengagement may be their expression that they want to avoid any socio-emotional, relational process that may be challenging or feel uncomfortable. We are reminded of the Swahili wisdom saying, as quoted in Paula McClain's 2015 book entitled *Circling the Sun*, "A new thing is good, though it be a sore place."

Harvard psychologist Carol Dweck's popular book *Mindset: The New Psychology of Success* is an excellent secular resource that can help overcome this issue of stonewalling, which she calls "fixed mindset," the opposite of her "growth mindset" that represents having a curious, open mind willing to learn.[2] It is an easy, interesting, and empowering read. The goal is to continue to bring God's faithful grace to the community outside and inside the church. Every church is challenged to invite, welcome, and affirm closed-minded persons from various viewpoints into the open discussion of new possibilities.

Individuals and subgroups who actively resist proposed changes are problematic. To simplify, we examine two different types of resistive behaviors—overt and covert. A prime example of an *overt resistance* problem is when someone gets up, stomps, or huffs out during the sermon delivery. The best response to this situation comes from lay leaders and not the clergy, which helps prevent the pastor from being set up for a direct confrontation. A lay leader can talk with the disgruntled person (perhaps an opposition leader) to hear the complaint and offer better ways to involve the person in the process so that her or his voice is heard in a more constructive manner.

Another problematic behavior is *covert communication* among dissenters outside of planned decision-making processes. Every effort should be made to invite, include, and hear every voice in an open setting for all involved to hear. This may sound risky, and it may get contentious at times, but that is all part of the process that is expected to happen. Clandestine activity in a church will only perpetuate and probably exacerbate the disagreements, and thus increase the turmoil within the socio-emotional, relational system of the church body. Stating positions openly is better even if doing so only ends with an agreement to disagree at that moment. Social media can also pose a high-risk challenge to the work of considering changes, which unfortunately can be done by anyone and even anonymously. Such dissent will only incite others outside the church to escalate the process into a big fight, which changes it into something ugly and counterproductive. We know of churches where this has happened, and we highly recommend taking every precaution to guarantee that does not occur in your church's process.

Reverend Culver from WBCC regularly proclaimed, "Every voice must be heard." To accomplish that, collaborative effort is needed to develop structures and implement processes for open dialogue with the goal of mutual understanding. Although one can expect conflicts and perhaps adamant disagreements initially, some churches in our studies used effective communication guidelines in their processes. From those, we developed the Guidelines for Healthy Trust-Building Discussions below. These limit-setting suggestions provide assurance that the reconciliation and conflict transformation process can healthfully continue toward a positive outcome. The process of discernment is an essential developmental activity for churches. A church's teaching and utilization of a specific process of discernment will most likely come from a pastor's leading or at least with a pastor's sanctioning. We suggest that such leading is aimed at opening the mind to receive new learning experiences. Also, discernment always includes Scripture reading, prayer, and silence, listening for God's will to be revealed. Discernment is important for both the individual and group, and it should be used throughout the total process.

The need for such a guideline became apparent to us through observing churches that did not consistently enforce their communication guidelines. The lack of enforcement interfered with their planned learning, discussion, and decision-making process. Their divisive opinions were allowed to be expressed with blaming and animosity, which escalated the conflicts within their church bodies. Personal attacks resulted in both sides pointing their fingers and accusing those in the other camp: "They do not believe the Bible!" Such blame-game attacks are not beneficial in any Christian church. Unfortunately, this is a clear example of how things can get messy if conflicts are not dealt with in an effective, transformative manner with effective communication guidelines like the ones below.

Group Processing: A Few More Suggestions

The goal of intentionally structured, open, conflict-transforming gatherings is for participants to communicate their feelings easily and safely to build trust. Those meetings are the focus of the process before a final decision is made on a policy or action plan regarding the issue in question. When structured and managed well, such meetings can facilitate a common understanding and more agreement on how a church can deal with divisive, value-laden issues, which may prevent fighting or even a split in the

Guidelines for Healthy Trust-Building Discussions

• *Begin the way you want to end: trusting God, other, and self.* We start with all taking a deep breath. Then another. And another to relax. Continue slow, deep breathing while remaining silent. Then look around to see all who are present and acknowledge their presence with compassion. Look at each person with gratitude and the love of Christ in your heart, thinking, *I see you and am willing to hear you because I care about you, our church, and our community.* Trust that in this process all can encounter the holy in that sacred space as you welcome the Holy Spirit. (Note: Have water available for everyone—we all do our best when fully hydrated. Food is optional, although we do tend to like the people with whom we share food.)

• *Keep the focus on discerning God's will in the moment.* Make Scripture reading, contemplation/silence, and prayer an integral part of all your discernment, learning, and discussion processes. Trust God to be present in the written as well as spoken and unspoken words. This will help you to remain strong as you vulnerably open your minds and share your personal opinions and values, along with listening to others.

• *Be considerate of the process.* Trust that this conversation grows out of careful and thoughtful dialogue among your group: staff, leaders, and your whole working group (congregation). Accept that no one person possesses a monopoly on the truth. Know that this is a discernment process—not a competition—as all are acting in good faith with good intentions, following your guiding light of trusting God, other, and self.

• *Speak respectfully at all times.* Be respectfully open and kind in your reactions to others as they share. Abide by the limits of no personal attacks, condemnations, or ridicule allowed. Even when disagreeing, be civil, be polite, and expect the same from others.

• *Commit to confidentiality.* What you see, hear, and say stays within the group. Therefore, nothing will be shared on social media. Thus, you can trust that you are safe while sharing personal opinions and deeply held values.

• *Be calm and cooperative, and empathize.* Remain curious and open to learning as you seek to be relational and peaceful without assuming controversy or conflict. Empathize, asking yourself what the speaker may be feeling emotionally before you respond. Allow time for all voices to be heard and valued. Focus on remaining calm while waiting during times of silence as you listen for and trust God's will throughout the process.

• *Be patient and collaborative.* Listen without interrupting and embrace questions as a means of seeking understanding rather than challenging. Trust that your statements will be heard and will receive consideration from others. Remember that this is not a debate; it is a discernment process, a series of steps before arriving at a mutually agreed upon conclusion. Also know that it takes time for people to gain a new understanding, some more than others.

• *Be faithful and trustworthy.* Be honest while participating in the spiritual discernment process, and share your conclusions at the meeting, not in the parking lot, in hallways, on the telephone, or on social media. Trust that in due time the best ending will come for the glory of God.

congregation. The larger question is how to function as the body of Christ in your community. A healthy decision-making process can help a congregation improve its outreach and mission ministries, including reaching out to marginalized individuals and families.

Trauma victims can be retraumatized by anything that might connect to their traumatic memory. Therefore, all discernment process discussions must include trauma sensitivity through developing a safe place with safeguard expectations. Healthy boundaries help prevent any harm as individuals share their personal experiences in past dealings with that issue in the church. Again, your expectations for best, kind behavior should be mutually agreed upon before starting any discussion process. Our suggested guidelines can ensure a place where people can agree to disagree, at least for the moment, and maintain their relationships with each other and the church. Consistently enforced communication monitoring and guidance are essential for keeping conversations constructive and not negative, and from attacking or condemning others. In general, the process can involve a combination of small-group and large-group interactions, with the focus on maintaining space for a safe and healthy environment where vulnerable, personal disclosure and dialogue can comfortably and safely take place.

In leading group processes, a simple technique can be valuable in drawing out quiet individuals' opinions. The group facilitator can say in the latter half of the discussion time, "Now we want to hear from those who have not already spoken." A variation of that is, "Now we want to hear from others who have a different viewpoint from what has been expressed so far."

One way to draw more people into the discernment process is to have small-group meetings in homes. There are two requirements for doing this: (1) respected church members who volunteer to host a small group and (2) a group leader who is skilled in planning/structuring and managing group processes. The leader can be a layperson, and for some the meetings may be more appealing if the leader is lay. Regardless, we recommend a support person be present to back up that leader to ensure all the interaction goes well. Also, having someone in charge of refreshments and hospitality can set the right tone. A lack of childcare may prohibit some from attending. A convenient option is to provide childcare at the church rather than in the house where the meeting is being held. The value of in-home meetings is that they function as a powerful social magnet, attracting more participants than even the best-planned meeting inside church walls.

One meeting we observed was in an elderly couple's home. The couple was financially well-off, living on Country Club Lane. They did not participate in many church activities, let alone the running of the church, but were longtime, respected members. This home gathering was well-attended (we expect that some participants mostly wanted to see their house). Participating church members filled the large living room, and folding chairs from the church allowed the whole group (eighteen) to sit during the discussion. The host couple did not have any responsibilities other than opening their door to the church for this one-hour meeting. No snacks or drinks were provided at that meeting, nor did they provide childcare, but no children were present. One lay leader facilitated the discussion of the issue using a flip chart. The pastor was the backup person. The meeting was primarily a presentation of the proposed change and information pertaining to it. More sophisticated audio-visual aids could be used (easier in some homes than others) as fit the topic of the meeting. All participants also had the opportunity to ask questions or express views of their own. The atmosphere was casual and relaxed. All participants exhibited good behavior throughout, and all interaction was friendly and meaningful. Afterward the church leaders and the couple hosting all agreed the meeting was effective and met its purpose well. This church had a few other house meetings scheduled in other homes to discern the best response for the church.

Invitations to in-home meetings can acknowledge that participants will hold a mixture of opinions. Preregistration is not mandatory but can help ensure that the meeting place is not overfull. No one should be excluded, so if the number of registrants grows too large, another meeting time and place can be added. Preregistration also gives the leaders an idea of how divergent participants' opinions may be. Although single meetings are the easiest to pull off, stark differences among the participants on specific issues may necessitate a lengthier process of three to six meetings. Multiple meetings can defuse the tension as they provide more time to transform the conflicts into a workable agreement on the question being addressed.

Every meeting should start with an understanding that all are not necessarily going to agree, and that the church's decision or position on the issue will neither be determined nor finalized in that meeting. Also, all participants are expected to covenant and commit to the trust-building discussion guidelines above. Reviewing those expectations is a good way to start.

Finally, a neutral icebreaker activity at the beginning can ensure everyone present knows their voice is to be heard as each takes a turn. An example is, "In one sentence answer, 'What is your hobby or what have you been spending your time doing?'"

In all their large, open learning/discussion sessions, church leaders must plan and manage their time well to allow ample time for all to have their say. They also must establish a plan that facilitates the participants' communication and interaction using a variety of group activities that help address the issue being discerned. Leaders can be creative, with the focus on the individuals being served—the process participants. Outside presenters should be held accountable to accommodate limitations on presentation time to ensure ample time for discussion. Time limits are critical, as presentations without time for discussion might function more as a divisive exercise that can decrease trust.

Another technique to elicit more involvement is to change from deciding (voting) to surveying in the earlier phase of the process. An advantage of the earlier surveying is that it provides an opportunity for self-expression by asking each to explain their position in writing (see the prototype in appendix B). Those survey participants' shared preferences or position responses could be used in the leaders' planning of how to draw all members' viewpoints into the discernment process. The data could also be used in the planning and structuring of upcoming open gatherings to build trust within the church community.

Moreover, it may invite, energize, and activate those who have taken a polar or extreme stonewall position to become more engaged during the discernment and decision-making process. Invariably, it requires church participants to put thought into articulating their personal responses to the issue at hand.

As you see, we have many options for gathering, becoming better acquainted, and discussing moral questions, controversial issues, and social initiatives. You are encouraged to be confident, creative, and collaborative in working on these matters as leaders to facilitate your congregation's progress in developing respect, trust, equity, and inclusion in our pluralistic society.

NOTES

1. Daniel Buttry, Sharon Buttry, et al., "Training for Conflict Transformation Trainers," Buttry Center for Peace and Nonviolence (Shawnee, KS: Central Seminary, August 7–16, 2018). See also Daniel Buttry, *Peace Warrior: A Memoir from the Front* (Macon, GA: Mercer University, 2012), 144, 238.

2. Carol S. Dweck, *Mindset: The New Psychology of Success—How We Can Fulfill Our Potential* (New York: Ballantine, 2016).

8

Other Voices: Companions on the Journey

It is time to put our money where our mouths are. We have been talking about the way that an elastic, adaptive church trusts the voices of others—even voices of disagreement and diversity. We acknowledge that as your authors, we are white, male, heterosexual Christians in a Christianized and powerful Western country. Let's be honest—you hear from people like us all the time. So, in the coming pages, we want to highlight the voices of people who are not like us. While interviewing and participating in the congregational work we have discussed, we have met incredible leaders and servants of God. They include women, persons of color, and of different ages who do not necessarily agree with us. We include the voices of LGBTQ+ persons. For confidentiality, we have removed names and identifying descriptors such as race. Some of these voices have experienced incredible pain in conversations like the ones we have been discussing. Please hold their holy stories with the honor they deserve.

 VOICE 1: Cisgender male, a middle-aged clergyperson in a mainline denomination, sexual orientation unascertained

The movement of including LGBTQ persons in every aspect of faith community life and ordained ministry has reached an irreversible point. The earthquake has happened, the tidal wave has hit, though the apex of the wave remains offshore and moving everyone's direction. There will be no dry, high ground. Every church will face the issue except those who respond with denial and avoidance.

This is the analogy I use for such a dramatic and ubiquitous change in US churches. It is a cultural shift that will ripple and echo throughout the global faith community. The question is not which churches will face this change, but when. Only churches that navigate LGBTQ inclusion successfully will make it through the twenty-first century—and half of those that do will still not survive. And this is the point: the decline of US churches, Catholic and Protestant alike, is the result of churches' general refusal to adapt on many levels. Getting LGBTQ inclusion right is essential and yet not enough. There is a substantive correlation: churches that cannot reframe dogmatic language or think critically about morality in a pluralistic culture are also unable to accommodate broader thinking on human sexuality.

To be sure, there are important words and actions that ministers should lead with despite the repercussions. But the onus of real progress lies squarely on the shoulders of the faith community's lay leadership. The roadblocks and deadlocks in the church are, more often than not, due to a conflicted membership that cannot navigate their value differences. Members who have served together for decades are hard-pressed to say things that could jeopardize these relationships. Well-meaning church members who wish to advocate for LGBTQ inclusion are reluctant to speak openly and risk offending long-standing church members. Worse, many members want to protect church revenue by quite intentionally avoiding offending "giving" members with the threatening language of inclusion.

Risking overgeneralization, there are three main paths churches can/will take. (1) Press forward with LGBTQ inclusion while being prepared to lose members and make the necessary fiscal adjustment to revenue changes. (2) Condemn the LGBTQ movement and stifle genuine inquiry and healthy conversation, ironically paving the way to closure or a church split. (3) Solicit trained outside assistance for conducting respectful communication. This will be led by mediation and communication experts (paid clergy are often also politically limited in facilitating highly sensitive conversations with their own congregations). With help, members might speak candidly in safe spaces and effectively listen to opposing values. Such a protocol requires financial investment and takes time. It is a significant and planned investment, not a one-time conversation after church. [Note: We strongly agree with his emphasis that it is an ongoing process.]

The challenge for churches is within both the context of the human sexuality debate and the broader context of regressive church habits that prevent authentic speaking, listening, and discovery. Unless congregants take the bold step of inviting and participating in guided, vulnerable conversations, the future is not in their hands. The tidal wave of inclusion is coming; yea, even now it is at the door.

 VOICE 2: Cisgender female, a late-middle-aged layperson in a mainline denomination, heterosexual

As I sit and type this in 2022 and reflect on all that our congregation has gone through in the last few years, I can't help but wish I had done at least one thing differently. We did not start our discussion on the LGBTQ community in a good place. We were a church that had "agreed to disagree" on many issues. The LGBTQ community acceptance became an issue upon which we could no longer agree to disagree. A church leader disclosed their identity as an LGBTQ person to other leaders but was not ready to "come out" publicly. The person felt unwelcome and left the church. When the rest of the congregation found out, there were many hurt feelings, and the church council began a process to determine next steps. I often wish that we had handled the situation differently, and perhaps we would not have had to go through the painful events. But then we wouldn't be where we are now.

We weren't in a good place. We had a pastor who was more conservative than many in our church. We had some individuals who thought they ran the church, and the pastor was trying to make everyone happy. We had services that were "fine," but nothing that would make you not want to miss them. And the LGBTQ issue shook us to the core.

We were divided instantly. The odd thing was that it was the older people who were more open to the issue and the younger ones who tended to be more conservative. So, when half of the congregation left, we were left with very few workers.

But that is what turned out to be the beautiful thing that happened. People who had never been the key workers of the church stepped forward to do jobs that they had never tried before. They also were happy to be doing them, and the congregation was grateful for their service. Everyone seemed to recognize that we might not survive as a church, and they wanted the church to be successful.

Our denomination sent us an interim minister who strongly believed that there was nothing in the Bible that said that a loving, committed LGBTQ relationship was a sin. This affirmed what many of us believed and created good discussions with those who didn't agree with him. He validated us in a way we really needed at the time.

The complaining that had gone on in our church is gone. Congregants seem grateful for the work being done. One man in the church reported that someone had come to him complaining about something relatively unimportant, and he put his arm around her and said, "After all we have been through, is this really worth worrying about?" She smiled and said that he was right. This is real progress!

We have a new pastor who was asked in the interviewing process if he would officiate an LGBTQ wedding. His response was that he would have to get the council's permission to marry a couple in the church, but if the church wouldn't allow that, he would marry them outside the church. He is very solid in his biblical belief that all are welcome, and he would marry them.

We have not made a final decision on the issue of LGBTQ marriage, but I believe the pastor is leading us in that direction. It still won't be easy, but I believe it will come.

On a personal note, I have often worried about an LGBTQ person who left the church. I have been able to make contact with them, and they have found a church that welcomes them for who they are. They are happy there. This was what I needed to hear in order to put the past behind me and look to the future.

 VOICE 3: Cisgender female, a late-middle-aged layperson, sexual orientation unascertained

My involvement as part of a small working group tasked with determining how best to involve the entire church community in a process for the church to determine its stance on same-gender marriage was one of the more profound experiences of my life. It felt profound because I was part of a community process in moving forward with what I believe to be one of the most consequential social justice concerns of our time. It also felt profound because of the wide diversity of views within our small group. I was challenged as to how to stay in conversation while maintaining full respect for other views and listening with my full self.

Personally, I experienced the following:

- frustration with the congregation's DNA of, in my opinion, lack of boldness in addressing social justice concerns and a "don't ask, don't tell" mentality on this one.

- fear and interior conflict about how much of my personal story to reveal to the working group or the congregation.

- frustration with the length of the process and the lack of follow-through on the part of a key leader for a significant period of time.

- passion and courage in using my voice along with that of another member of the working group to encourage the process not to stall and die out.

- patience with a very slow congregational process—making every effort to ensure that every member of the congregation had a voice and was encouraged and welcomed into the conversation—including the youth.

- frustration when a member of the working group did not participate in the church-wide planned opportunities for conversation.

- the constant presence of a beloved aunt in my heart (deceased some years ago) who was part of the LGBTQ community. I wanted to be part of a church community where she would have felt welcomed and safe.

I believe the following were the most significant factors in my church's process. (1) There was leadership from the pastor in initiating a church-wide opportunity for conversation following the Supreme Court ruling in 2015. (2) There was a more than gracious amount of time (two-plus years) for the entire process. (3) There was leadership from the church lay leaders. (4) We had an intentionally widely diverse working group and the dedication of that group. (5) I appreciated the reading of diverse resources by the working group. (6) We had multiple efforts and avenues of communication. (7) Once the work of the small working group was completed, there was a specific beginning and ending point for the church-wide conversations. Finally, (8) a church-wide session that involved the following stories of church members who either were part of the LGBTQ community themselves or whose family member was:

> *"I don't believe I would have wanted for anything to be different in the process other than to not have had the lengthy time gap when the working group stalled due to lack of leader follow-through."*

"I moved at the very end of the church-wide process. My hope, however, is that the experience of this process shifted the church's DNA so that there might be more courage to address other social justice concerns. I also hope that in time there might be more movement on this one so that without a doubt, LGBTQ persons would feel free to participate fully in all aspects of church life as their authentic selves."

"I will always hold a memory of a letter I received from a member of the working group after I had shared some of my personal story with the group in a vulnerable way. The member was on the opposite end of the spectrum from me in terms of our views, but her letter was kind and supportive of me as a person. During this process, in many ways like this one, I experienced the beloved community."

 VOICE 4: Cisgender female, a middle-aged clergyperson in a mainline denomination, heterosexual

The day before the Supreme Court declared gay marriage legal, we put up an outdoor banner with this invitation: "All Are Welcome, Come Just as You Are!" Sitting in my car at the red light across from the banner the next day, I realized, That sign means something different today. Before I could get into the building, our lay leader called me and nervously asked, "How do you plan to respond to gay marriage?"

A special guidance team was created to partner with me and the church council to help navigate a congregational process. A key element in the process was giving everyone a voice. Each person would be listened to and respected regardless of their position. This immediately presented the challenges ahead as some said, "Yes, we are all in," or, "No, we shouldn't be discussing this at all." Also helpful to the process was our commitment to open communication and transparency.

At each step of the process, the guidance team would reconvene to evaluate how things were going, what more was needed, and what step to take next. Many of our members needed opportunities to learn more about same-gender-attracted persons and couples. They needed an opportunity to ask questions, to hear from a same-gender couple, and to learn from someone in the medical field. The conversations and opportunities were helpful but also challenging. With each guest speaker or shared group experience, we debriefed and asked for feedback.

The guidance team felt like we were still missing feedback from folks who had not attended the sessions. We created a survey with room for comments and sent it to everyone. We did receive responses from those we were concerned about. Following this step, the team discerned we were ready to move forward with creating a proposal to welcome, include, and marry all persons. The proposal was sent to each member prior to a special business meeting and luncheon.

We intentionally hosted lunch and the meeting after worship. Congregants were seated at round tables in smaller groups. The guidance team presented the proposal and then gave time for response. This was a bit of a risk, but the reward was great. Individuals who originally said, "We shouldn't be talking about this," or "We will leave the church," got up and shared something different. One gentleman shared how our congregation was the only church that would marry a Hispanic man and a Black woman in the 1970s. He shared his regret about being so exclusive at the beginning of the process. Another woman got up and said she had been the judge and gatekeeper for God long enough and was giving it up. Many others shared that loving all our neighbors was more important than anything else, according to Scripture! When folks were finished sharing, we presented the proposal again and took a vote. Only one person voted no, and another removed their membership. Overall, there was a sigh of relief and joy in the room.

VOICE 5: Cisgender female, a retirement-aged layperson in a mainline denomination, heterosexual

I was part of our church's process from the beginning to the end. Parts of the process were all positive: the adult Sunday school class's work on formulating and promoting the discussion to include the whole church; the parts that were open to and thus involved the whole church; and the church leadership's decision that involved the whole church. However, I was on the task force committee, and I am critical of our congregation's process.

The first meeting of the committee was great, as we all shared our own stories. One woman told us that her sister was a lesbian. After that first meeting, our committee got really boring, as the assigned books were really dry reading. The council had decided it would be lay-led, which influenced the extended period of time before the whole church became involved. It was way too slow, and I think that had a negative effect on our process. I think people got rigidly entrenched in their positions long before we opened the process to include the whole church.

It could have been more positive if there had not been many months where nothing was done, and when the committee did meet, there was a lot of absenteeism. And the committee's process lacked congenial conversation. Also, the extended time period allowed some contentious people within the church to form their own group to advocate and mobilize against our church becoming inclusive. That was where our process broke down.

Then changes came—a new lay leader helped us develop a plan to move forward. And the committee developed a really positive experience for the whole church to participate. But the divisive faction had already formed. That led to our outcome after the vote of a significant number leaving. That was very sad—sad for them and sad for all the people in the church.

VOICE 6: Cisgender female, a young adult clergyperson in a mainline denomination, heterosexual

When considering the process of becoming a welcoming and affirming church, we quickly realized that for us, a status of welcoming and affirming might reduce our ability to welcome all as we do today. Often people ask, "Well, Pastor, since your church is such a welcoming church, why don't you have a sign in front of the church that says this church is welcoming and affirming?" This question makes sense. We [pastors] have married same-sex couples, and we have same-sex couples as active members. While almost everybody in the church seems to love them, we know there are members who are not comfortable with the idea yet. Should these members be excluded for not being ready yet? We believe it is possible to welcome, accept, and value each other without being fully on board with lifestyle or life choices. How we handle such a conversation and process matters. If a church is welcoming, anyone should feel welcome in it. Just because somebody is not comfortable with the lifestyle does not immediately mean that he or she cannot at least tolerate it.

I will never forget what one member said as I called to check if she was attending our first same-sex wedding. She said, "Pastor, I have no problem with their choice, but I'm not ready yet. I'll probably get them a gift and a card, but I'm not ready to attend their wedding." This was a sincere response. Clearly, a few members are still not comfortable with same-gender loving relationships yet.

We are open and welcoming and affirming to an extent, but we are still avoiding making a decision. We are welcoming and also inclusive. On our leadership teams and committee boards, we have young, old, LGBTQIA+, straight, and multiple races participating. Everyone is included. I do not see our church making a decision on this matter anytime soon. Here is why: my church is a melting pot—we all show each other mutual respect and get along well. We are a group of loving people who care for each other. It does not matter our lifestyle or beliefs.

To us, we have chosen a form of inclusivity that does not exclude one group while including others. I believe it is important that both the people who are not ready and those who are have more opportunities to sit at the same table and learn from each other. The more they hang out together, the higher the chance of finding common ground and relating better to each other.

Finally, our intercultural DNA urges us to respect the lived beliefs and cultures of our sisters and brothers. When we invite people to join our congregation, we do not invite them to come to be like us, believe like we do, and live life the way we do. We instead invite them to come just as they are with their flaws and qualities, with their lifestyle and beliefs. In this way, we are all constantly shaping each other in respectful and inclusive ways. Our common goal is to love one another.

You have just read the stories individuals are telling about their churches and their processes, their methods for dealing with same-sex relationships and marriage. They also revealed some personal feelings as well as the socio-emotional expressions their congregation has experienced in their process of adaptation. We deeply appreciate each one's generous contribution to our story. They have provided insights and guidance for us all, as does our next chapter, which maps out general guides for each faith community journey.

9

The Path Ahead

The most recent statistics show that 7 percent of the population self-identifies as LGBTQ+.[1] Since this is an upward trend, churches will do well to respond adaptively. Our hope is that the observations and conclusions in this book provide information for understanding and dealing with the unprecedented diversity of persons living in our neighborhoods today.

Our three composite churches, like other faith communities, revealed their work at maintaining active, peaceful relationships and interactions among their members. Our observations and comparisons are intended to mesh with the church-at-large purposes of bonding together for the sake of ministry to each other, as well as for building up the body of Christ. Applying this information can help a church cocreate a healthy community in accordance with the will of the loving and gracious Holy Spirit of God.

We must reiterate that while this singular issue is significant in the conversations of many congregations, our hope is that these principles and guidelines will be helpful for building trust amid any controversy the church might face. These strategies were developed from the examination of multiple churches' lives through the lenses of holistic human interaction, alterity, systems theory, and orthopathy, offering a means for gaining insights into understanding and dealing with the reality of divisiveness.

We observed patterns and processes of attending, listening, and reconciling trust-building practices in churches as they responded to major societal shifts. From an authentic, power-sharing stance, we learned a new, empowered, empathetic way of understanding and interacting. This is a worshipful work way of being church—a way of meeting new people while engaging the divine. This trust-building process will enable the disruptive innovation of cocreating a heterogeneous, pluralistic, loving group of diverse individuals who are open to respecting, inviting, including, affirming, and collaborating with all. We have offered tools throughout the book to support trust-building processes, such as our Cycle of Building Trust Model and Packing List of guidelines in chapter 5 and our individual and group communication guidelines in chapter 7.

In completing all four phases of trust-building, we invite, welcome, include, support, affirm, and collaborate with the other: people new to our congregational work in our diverse community. As we welcome, wonder, worship, and work together, we experience meeting the Holy Spirit and connecting with the divine. By accomplishing peace within, peace between, peace among, and peace with God, we can continue this cycle perpetually for social justice and the glory of God.

When church participants live out their faith in this manner, they join in what has been called "the divine dance."[2] This dance is accomplished not only by focusing on interrelating with God and God's love, acceptance, and grace toward all of God's creation but also focusing on relating justly and graciously with one another both within their church system and in their community at large. With this, Christian churches can affirm the worth of each individual and continue as viable social institutions thriving in their communities by bringing the love and grace of God to earth—"Thy kingdom come"—with participants in the churches doing the will of God "on earth as it is in heaven."

Don't Forget. . .

To remind us of things we shouldn't forget, our mothers used to pin a note on our jackets as we ran out the door. A few reminders as you head out on your journey:

1. Every pastor, every lay leader, every group, and every faith community is unique. The principles and guidelines in this volume must be adapted to fit the context. Beware: what works for one may have the worst outcome for another.

2. Remember that a decision-making process takes time—much time. We found that a successful decision-making process (one that resulted in a specific decision with general consensus) takes approximately a two-year time span (plus or minus six months). We do not advise rushing the process, dragging out the process, or trying to avoid it.

3. A decision-making process must be intentionally approached and planned with a long-term perspective that seeks and utilizes good discernment practices from beginning to end for clergy and laypersons alike. We are aware of one congregation that initiated a rushed process that put the whole church system through an exceedingly difficult time as it escalated prior conflicts within that church body. Their process ended with turmoil boiling within the church, which culminated in a break-up—the exodus of many members and leaders. These are not simple decisions that we make. Biblical interpretation, community policy, and the real lives of those in the congregation impact the way we talk about and discuss these significant issues.

4. Our final gem is best summarized by the advice Rev. Cliff Matthews Jr. received from his grandmother: "Begin the way you want to end."[3]

Our world is ever-changing. Church leaders, including pastors, must not only be aware of those changes, but they also must deal with them directly as they actively discern God's will in reference to the lives of the people—all the people. Church leaders need self-awareness of their emotions and empathic awareness of the feelings of all others. This awareness will best help them to communicate, interact, and interrelate with the people in their communities in a power-sharing, egalitarian manner. All this work can be done with not only the welfare of current congregants but also the church's outreach to their community in mind by way of evangelism and social justice services. It requires including and embracing alterity—openness to otherness—and listening to them with empathy and compassion, rather than moving to rescue them. We must remember that the other may perceive us as judgmental persecutors as that is the stereotype of Christians. When we can act with humility, acceptance, and compassion, this warm welcoming openness enables and empowers serving and collaborating with all, in addition to sharing worship, prayer, music, and Communion. In doing that, we can stay connected to the Holy Spirit of Christ in our ministries. Without an open, growth mindset, a church could be at risk of decline and even extinction. Our prayer is that this book is a constructive aid to each church system's process of serving, teaching, preaching, and staying abundantly alive, connected, and listening to the Spirit and gracious will of the triune God: Creator, Christ, and Holy Comforter.

NOTES

1. Jeffrey M. Jones, "LGBT Identification in U.S. Ticks Up to 7.1%," Gallup, February 17, 2022, https://news.gallup.com/389792/lgbt-identifictation-ticks-up.aspx.

2. Molly T. Marshall, *Joining the Dance: A Theology of the Spirit* (Valley Forge, PA: Judson, 2003), 7, 52; and Richard Rohr, *The Divine Dance: The Trinity and Your Transformation* (New Kensington, PA: Whitaker House, 2016).

3. Cliff Matthews Jr., Zoom interview with authors, March 20, 2022.

Afterword

Hope for the Future

Worried.
Distrust.
Divided.

We began our exploration together with such words at the front of our minds, asking if a model exists for churches that allows them to survive, navigate, and perhaps even thrive amid polarized worldviews. The question was not simply a detached cognitive exercise, but one born of our own pain and the pain of others whom we know well. As we have discussed churches in crisis, images of very real congregations, leaders, and people came to the fore. The academic description of a purple church also carries with it memories of Black, blue, and purple bruises, caused by divisiveness and anger that found their way into the church. Some congregations we know well lost members through the processes we describe. Other members stayed but found themselves disillusioned with their leadership or their congregations. In some cases, individuals were shocked at how differently their pew mates and longtime fellow members interpreted Scripture or felt about certain political issues. They thought they were in a church with like-minded believers as blue or red as they were, but they were shocked to find out that their church was more purple than they realized!

Listen.
Trust.
Grow.

Along the way, other words have come into play—holy and hopeful words and concepts and images and stories of God at work among us. We know that Barnes's concern with which we began—for the "churches in the center"—will not be solved by one simple book. It will continue to take work—your good and holy work—and an openness to the work of God in your midst. But we believe that this work will not be in vain! In fact, we believe that there is hope that congregations such as yours can witness the power of God to overcome even the most rigid political divisiveness.

Polity, process, and preaching are all keys to the existence of a healthy, elastic, purple church. We have offered models and lessons shared with family systems theory and healthy socio-emotional relational functioning. But at the heart of it all is *trust.* We must trust that God is at work in, through, and among God's people, even in these churches in the center.

We know there will still be a place for blue churches and red churches. They are crucial voices in the church's ongoing task of both progressing and conserving. In their own ways, they may become or already are adaptive, elastic congregations that understand the value of alterity. They open their eyes to the truth in the next pew and celebrate those differences. Red, blue, or purple, they are open to the otherness of their friends and neighbors. In essence, they say, "I don't want to be around *only* people who are like me. I want to be in a church in which we represent a range of ideologies and appreciate and value those differences. I trust that God is at work in those differences." This can be a value of conservatives or of progressives, but it is not a presumption of either.

We reserve our final word for those who have engaged in a form of this purple church project. You have committed to this vision of an elasticized ecclesiology that stretches across the boundaries that cable news and your social media feed insist cannot be crossed. You believe that we are better off alongside those who do not lock step with our own theology or politics. You are as committed to this idea of purpleness as you are to your own ideologies. To be clear, this is not every church's calling.

But it is a calling. This call is an ordained blessing by God to be something that many in our culture insist cannot exist— *should* not exist. Such work takes patience and commitment and, of course, a lot of trust. But you do not do this work alone. Others feel called and ordained to the same work—a network of purpleness across denominations and geography. You stand on the shoulders of the great cloud of witnesses in the legacy of congregations who have navigated similar waters over the generations. And there is always—eternally—the presence of the Holy Spirit of God in our midst: empowering, discerning, inviting. Our hope for the future.

Appendix A

An Example Sermon Crafted to Evoke Trust

This sermon was a part of a series with the explicit goal of teaching trust content. Titled "Trust Me! Trusting God and Others in an Untrusting World," it asks the congregation to see the body of Christ (1 Corinthians 12) amid a potentially divisive controversy within the church.

I started to notice the geese flying south for the winter last week. It's always a sign of winter when you see that recognizable V pattern flying through the air and hear that honking as they communicate with one another.

Scientists have told us that there are a couple of reasons why they fly in a V formation. The first is that it builds trust in the flock. When the birds fly hundreds of miles together, the V gives them what scientists call visual assurance. Basically, they can keep track of each other better. If they were flying together in a random mob, it would be harder to know if Kyle the goose is still with them or what happened to Mary goose. They build trust in the flock when they are assured that they can see each other and keep track of each other.

Maybe we should learn from the geese!

For we live in a culture in which trust is increasingly eroding.

How would you answer this question: "Generally speaking, would you say that most people can be trusted or that you can't be too careful in dealing with people?"

This is the question that researchers have asked Americans since 1972. And they have recorded those answers for decades.

The results of the General Social Survey show a stark drop in the level of trust within our culture, eroding significantly in the last fifty years.[1] Interestingly, enough researchers over that time have also studied how religion plays a part in this topic. Do Christians trust more than non-Christians? Like a lot of research, it depends on how you ask the question, but many studies have shown that the Christian faith has absolutely no change in how much people trust each other!

And it shows. I think there is a significant mistrust in the way we interact with each other. If someone looks different or has a different way of living than we do, then we aren't sure we can trust them. We don't begin with an assumption of curiosity, but one of suspicion. If someone is like me, then they can be trusted. If they are not, they cannot. We have seen a rise in hate crimes, in race-related violence, in brazen comments, and in verbal attacks of the person on the street. When we see someone we don't know, we are more likely to mistrust them. On this anniversary of the death of Matthew Shepard, a victim of a hate crime just because a group of teens couldn't handle someone who was different from them, we have to ask if we are much different than we were twenty years ago.

Eroded trust means eroded relationships and eroded communities, and the picture is clear.

The same scene plays itself out in the book of Corinthians. Corinth was located on an isthmus, so there were ports on both sides of the city. The community and the church were bombarded all the time with new cultures, new ideas, and new people. For a lot of the church, this was terrifying. There were so many "others," people who were "different from me." It was hard work to be in community, and the Corinthians didn't do very well. The Jewish Christians tried to make sure that anyone who was not Jewish became Jewish first: "If you are going to belong, you have to be like me first." Some Christians, those who tended to be richer and more powerful, reacted by staging their own "members-only Communion" in which they showed up early and were already drunk when the rest of the church showed up. They trusted "people like me" but not someone who was different. They distrusted the "other" in their midst and tried to hide in enclaves just like them. Even within the church, trust had eroded, relationship had eroded. And for Paul, it was clear that faith had eroded.

But Paul had a remedy: in the face of common distrust, Paul preached a radical trust!

Most of us have probably heard of the metaphor of the body of Christ. It is one of Paul's favorites. But he did not make it up. In fact, it was a common metaphor for his time. Philosophers and politicians used it as a metaphor for the *polis* or the city-state. Everyone was a part of the body. Everyone had a part to play. But the common use of the metaphor was hierarchical. The governors were the head, and the commoners were the feet or the legs. Everyone had a place, but some had a special place while others were mostly cogs in the wheel.

Paul took that metaphor and applied it to the church in revolutionary ways. He suggests in this passage that we are all in this together, and that everyone has an equal part to play. He tosses out the idea of the hierarchy and instead suggests that the parts that we call inferior or dishonorable are actually just as important, if not indispensable! *Every* voice matters. *Every* person has a role in the body. We are *all* in this *together*, and no one is more important than anyone else!

Yung Suk Kim is a Pauline scholar who specializes in the study of Paul's correspondence to Corinth. He suggests that what Paul does here is pretty radical. Many have used the metaphor to stress unity, but Kim actually suggests that unity is a double-edged sword. "Who gets to define unity? Who or what will we be unified around?" The goal of unity is often homogeneity. We need to be unified, so you need to line up behind me. This is basically what the Corinthians were saying to each other.

But Kim suggests that Paul didn't stress unity as much as he did diversity. Unity is a top-down, hierarchical definition. The Nazi Party was unified! Unity is not always a good thing! But, according to Kim, what Paul was actually up to was teaching diversity. Every voice matters as much as the next one's voice! He says it this way:

> *Challenging the traditional vision of Christian life as a lonely journey on the part of one who leaves family and community for a heavenly city . . . an ethic of diversity aims at responsible living together in mutual care. Paul offers a vision of living in diversity, respecting differences, engaging the other with self-critical awareness, and caring for the other in solidarity and for creation in wonder.*[2]

Instead of homogeneity, Paul stressed radical diversity. And of course, to get to that, it required radical trust. Paul finished this chapter on body diversity by suggesting, "Now I will show you a more excellent way." Perhaps you have heard that more excellent way:

> *Love is patient, love is kind. It does not envy, it does not boast, it is not proud. It does not dishonor others, it is not self-seeking, it is not easily angered, it keeps no record of wrongs. Love does not delight in evil but rejoices with the truth. It always protects, always trusts, always hopes, always perseveres.*
> *[1 Corinthians 4-7 NIV]*

Radical body. Radical diversity. Radical trust.

And Paul's remedy for the Corinthians is the same remedy for us. Radical trust yields radical diversity yields radical faith.

I used to think it was the other way around. In fact, I have been studying this concept of trust for the last few years as a part of my DMin work. When I began, I thought my job was simple. I was going to teach you all how to trust. I would read the Bible to you, and you would trust God more, and then as a result, you would trust each other more. I was going to lead trust. I was going to evoke trust. I was going to make you all trust each other!

In fact, I am still transforming on this. I read 1 Corinthians 12:13 this week and thought the same thing again. See where it says, "You are *made* to drink of the Spirit." I was right there with Paul: I am going to *make* you all drink of the Spirit. I am going to *make* you all trust God. And then as a result, you will trust each other.

But, of course, Paul says it happens the other way around. We learn to trust each other, to learn from each other in community, to be the diverse body of Christ. It wasn't until I was sitting down with a group of church members, reading this passage together, that I realized what it actually said. "You are *made* to drink of the Spirit." Not *you are forced* to drink of the Spirit, but you are *created* to drink of the Spirit. That's who you are. The beauty of true Christian community is that we trust each other. Then God becomes real in our midst. There is a bluegrass song written by Shorty Sullivan and Thomas Coley and a version sung by Rhonda Vincent that teaches that if "you don't love God, if you don't love your neighbor." Neighbor love, neighbor trust, is not a top-down, hierarchical business. God will teach me and I will teach you. Instead, we learn it together. We learn it with each other.

I learn to trust you by serving beside you in Haiti. You learn to trust me by eating lunch with me on Tuesdays. I learn to trust you by listening to your wisdom on Wednesday nights. You learn to trust me by listening to what I have to say on Sunday mornings. We trust each other by coming to Sunday school and having congregational conversations and small groups together.

Your voice matters! But we don't believe it. The group I met with this week admitted this is hard because we don't believe that we are worthy of trust. We are broken people. Imperfect people. We live in a world of constant self-conscious, self-judging, mistrust of self. As one person said, "Most days I think that my part in the body of Christ is to be a hair on a mole." Paul says, "Yeah. We all are. We all feel that way." That's why we are so insistent that everyone be like us, so that it makes us feel less self-conscious of our brokenness. But again, Paul reminds us it is the love of Christ that makes us whole. Like someone else said this week, "I wish everyone could believe this."

I told you earlier that there are two reasons geese fly in formation. The first is trust. The second is efficiency. It helps save energy. Each goose gets a chance to lead for a while, taking the turn at the front. The formation helps them draft off the lead goose. One works hard for a while to make it easier for the rest. When they get tired, the next goose takes over and the lead goose drops back. If one gets sick or injured, another goose stays with it. Mutual trust. Shared community. Not because they did efficiency studies and crunched the numbers and this way worked the best! Because it's the way they were made. Trust and community.

It's the way we were made. Created to care for each other and trust each other.

NOTES

1. Pew report, https://www.pewresearch.org/politics/2019/07/22/the-state-of-personal-trust/.

2. Yung Suk Kim, *Christ's Body in Corinth: The Politics of a Metaphor* (Minneapolis: Fortress Press, 2008), 102.

3. "You Don't Love God If You Don't Love Your Neighbor" sung by Rhonda Vincent, written by Shorty Sullivan, Thomas Coley. Lyrics © Sony/ATV Music Publishing LLC, https://www.lyrics.com/lyric/4838365/Rhonda+Vincent/You+Don%27t+Love+God+If+You+Don%27t+Love+Your+Neighbor.

Appendix B

Suggested Survey Questions to Facilitate Your Congregation's Discernment Process

Please trust that your responses will be kept in the strictest of confidence (name not required).

1. If you believe this church should or should not be open, welcoming, and affirming of all persons, please share why and what that means to you. _____
   _____.
   _____
   _____

2. Do you feel the church should develop a statement that addresses our position on LGBTQ+ or same-sex weddings, particularly as it relates to membership or leadership? Please explain. _____
   _____
   _____
   _____

3. If a pastor of this church, through their calling as a minister of God, chose to marry a same-gender couple, would you support their decision? Why or why not? _____
   _____
   _____
   _____

4. The membership of this church is diverse but continues to serve together, unified by our vision and mission. Whatever the final decision from our discussions of this issue, are you willing to accept that decision and continue as a member of this church? Why or why not? _____

_____

_____

_____

_____

5. Research indicates that 4 to 7 percent of the American population identifies as lesbian, gay, bisexual, transgender, queer, or intersex. How can we best minister to all people, including persons who identify as LGBTQ+ or are different from most in other ways? _____

_____

_____

_____

_____

6. Is there specific language, behavior or a particular decision that would prohibit you from being or continuing to be a member of this church? Please explain your responses.

_____

_____

_____

_____

7. Do you have additional comments for the leadership team or pastoral staff leading this discussion not covered in the questions above? Please add comments below.

_____

_____

_____

_____

Bibliography

Ahlgrim, Ryan. "Three Reasons Why Gay Acceptance Has Been So Divisive in MC USA." *The Mennonite*, July 28, 2018. https://the mennonite.org/opinion/three-reasons-gay-acceptance-divisive-mc-usa/.

Allen, O. Wesley. *The Homiletic of All Believers: A Conversational Approach to Proclamation and Preaching*. Louisville: Westminster John Knox, 2005.

Allyn, Bobby. "Here Are 4 Key Points from the Facebook Whistleblower's Testimony on Capitol Hill." NPR.org. Updated October 5, 2021. https://www.npr.org/2021/10/05/1043377310/facebook-whistle blower-frances-haugen-congress.

Ammerman, Nancy T. "Congregation and Association: Rethinking Baptist Distinctives for a New Century." In *Baptists in the Balance: The Tension between Freedom and Responsibility*, edited by Everett C. Goodwin, 260–71. Valley Forge, PA: Judson, 1997.

———. "Priests and Prophets." In *Proclaiming the Baptist Vision: The Priesthood of All Believers*, edited by Walter B. Shurden, 55–62. Macon, GA: Smyth & Helwys, 1993.

Ammerman, Nancy T., Jackson W. Carroll, et al., eds. *Studying Congregations: A New Handbook*. Nashville: Abingdon, 1998.

Avilesbernal, Douglas, with Linda Triemstra Cook. *Welcoming Community: Diversity That Works*. Valley Forge, PA: Judson, 2016.

Barnes, M. Craig. "The Pastors I Worry About." *Christian Century*, January 4, 2017, 35.

Bartlett, David. Unpublished class notes via Matthew Sturtevant. Unpublished raw data, June 27, 2017.

Bonner, Timothy J. "Comparison of Four Midwest Congregations in Transition of Decision-Making on Same-Gender Marriage Using Bowen Family Systems Theory." DMin diss., Central Seminary, 2018.

———. "Your Church and Same-Gender Marriage—Part 1." Good Faith Media, January 4, 2021. https://goodfaithmedia.org/your-church-and -same-gender-marriage-part-1/.

———. "Your Church and Same-Gender Marriage—Part 2." Good Faith Media, January 5, 2021. https://goodfaithmedia.org/your-church-and -same-gender-marriage-part-2/.

Buttry, Daniel L. *Peace Warrior: A Memoir from the Front*. Macon, GA: Mercer University Press, 2012.

Buttry, Daniel, Sharon Buttry, et al. "Training for Conflict Transformation Trainers," Buttry Center for Peace and Nonviolence. Shawnee, KS: Central Seminary, August 7-16, 2018.

Bibliography

Cladis, George. *Leading the Team-Based Church: How Pastors and Church Staffs Can Grow Together into a Powerful Fellowship of Leaders.* San Francisco: Jossey-Bass, 1999.

Cleghorn, John. *Resurrecting Church: Where Justice and Diversity Meet Radical Welcome and Healing Hope.* Minneapolis: Fortress, 2021.

Dunkelman, Marc. "The Transformation of American Community." *National Affairs,* Summer 2011.

Dunning, David, Joanna E. Anderson, et al. "Trust at Zero Acquaintance: More a Matter of Respect Than Expectation of Reward." *Journal of Personality and Social Psychology* 107, no. 1 (2014): 122–41.

Dweck, Carol S. *Mindset: The New Psychology of Success—How We Can Fulfill Our Potential.* New York: Ballantine, 2016.

Ekman, Paul. *Moving toward Global Compassion.* San Francisco: Ekman, 2014.

———. *Emotions Revealed: Recognizing Faces and Feelings to Improve Communication and Emotional Life.* 2nd ed. New York: Owl, 2007.

Fowl, Stephen E., and L. Gregory Jones. *Reading in Communion.* Eugene, OR: Wipf and Stock, 1998.

Friedman, Edwin H., Margaret M. Treadwell, and Edward W. Beal. *A Failure of Nerve: Leadership in the Age of the Quick Fix.* Rev. 10th anniversary ed. New York: Church, 2017.

Goleman, Daniel. *Social Intelligence: The New Science of Human Relationships.* New York: Bantam, 2007.

Gushee, David, Brian McLaren, et al. *Changing Our Mind: The Landmark Call for Inclusion of LGBT Christians and Response to Critics.* 3rd ed. Canton, MI: Read the Spirit Books, 2019. [Note: This volume includes a study guide.]

Haidt, Jonathan. *The Righteous Mind: Why Good People Are Divided by Politics and Religion.* New York: Vintage Books, 2013.

Harris, Robert A. *Entering Wonderland: A Toolkit for Pastors New to a Church.* Lanham, MD: Rowman & Littlefield, 2014.

Hawley, Katherine. *Trust: A Very Short Introduction.* Oxford: Oxford University Press, 2012.

Herring, Hayim, and Terri Martinson Elton. *Leading Congregations and Nonprofits in a Connected World.* Lanham, MD: Rowman & Littlefield, 2017.

Hogan, Lucy Lind, and Robert Reid. *Connecting with the Congregation: Rhetoric and the Art of Preaching.* Nashville: Abingdon, 1999.

Jensen, Richard A. *Thinking in Story: Preaching in a Post-Literate Age.* Repr. ed. Lima, OH: CSS Publishing, 1995.

Jones, Jeffry M. "LGBT Identification Ticks Up to 7.1%." Gallup. February 17, 2022. https://news.gallup.com/poll/389792/lgbt-identification-ticks-up.aspx.

Kaveny, Cathleen. *Prophecy without Contempt: Religious Discourse in the Public Square.* Cambridge, MA: Harvard University Press, 2016.

Keller, Catherine. *On the Mystery: Discerning Divinity in Process*. Minneapolis: Fortress, 2008.

Kerr, Michael E. *Bowen Theory's Secrets: Revealing the Hidden Life of Families*. Kindle ed. New York: Norton, 2019.

———. *One Family's Story: A Primer on Bowen Theory*. Kindle ed. Washington, DC: Georgetown Family Center, 2003.

Kim, Grace Ji-Sun. *Invisible: Theology and the Experience of Asian American Women*. Minneapolis: Fortress, 2021

———. and Susan M. Shaw. *Intersectional Theology: An Introductory Guide*. Minneapolis: Fortress, 2018.

Kim, Yung Suk. *Christ's Body in Corinth: The Politics of a Metaphor*. Minneapolis: Fortress, 2008.

Lose, David J. *Preaching at the Crossroads: How the World and Our Preaching Is Changing*. Minneapolis: Fortress, 2014.

Marney, Carlyle. *Priests to Each Other*. Repr. ed. Macon, GA: Smyth and Helwys, 2001.

Marshall, Molly T. *Joining the Dance: A Theology of the Spirit*. Valley Forge, PA: Judson, 2003.

Martin, Colby. *Unclobber: Rethinking Our Misuse of the Bible on Homosexuality*. Louisville: Westminster John Knox, 2016.

Marty, Martin E. *Building Cultures of Trust*. Grand Rapids: Eerdmans, 2010.

McClure, John. *Other-wise Preaching: A Postmodern Ethic for Homiletics*. St. Louis, MO: Chalice, 2001.

Moltmann, Jürgen. *The Trinity and the Kingdom: The Doctrine of God*. Minneapolis: Fortress, 1993.

McLain, Paula. *Circling the Sun*. NY: Penguin Random House, 2015.

Moss, Otis. *Blue Note Preaching in a Post-Soul World: Finding Hope in an Age of Despair*. Louisville: Westminster John Knox, 2015.

Olson, Richard P., Ruth Lofgren Rosell, Nathan S. Marsh, and Angela Barker Jackson. *A Guide to Ministry Self-Care: Negotiating Today's Challenges with Resilience and Grace*. Lanham, MD: Rowman & Littlefield, 2018.

"Partisanship and Political Animosity in 2016." Pew Research Center, Washington, DC. (June 22, 2016). https://www.pewresearch.org/politics/2016/06/22/partisanship-and-political-animosity-in-2016/.

Richardson, Ronald W. *The Church in Transition: Three Talks on Bowen Family Systems Theory and Dealing with Change in the Church*. Kindle ed. CreateSpace, 2017.

Rohr, Richard. *The Divine Dance: The Trinity and Your Transformation*. New Kensington, PA: Whitaker House, 2016.

Rose, Lucy Atkinson. *Sharing the Word: Preaching in the Roundtable Church*. Louisville: Westminster John Knox, 2000.

Ryan, James R. *Doing Justice in a Purple Congregation*. Denver: Colorado Council of Churches, 2008.